2⁰⁰

THE MASTER OF SPACE AND TIME

Jeff Campbell of The Clean Team. The unrivaled master of modern home cleaning and organization. In San Francisco, Jeff and The Clean Team whip an entire house into shape in forty-two minutes flat. Nobody does it better. Nobody even comes close.

He knows the secrets of your home better than you do. The stuff you need. The stuff you don't. And he can find amazing places to put your stuff so it's right at hand if you really need it—but out of sight and out of your way.

What's the catch? Do it his way. No arguments. No discussions. No compromises.

Why? Because it works!

CLUTTER CONTROL

FOR THOSE WHO WOULD RATHER BE WINNING THE WAR AGAINST STUFF!

Look for Other Dell Books by
Jeff Campbell and The Clean Team

SPEED CLEANING
SPRING CLEANING

*PUTTING
YOUR HOME
ON A DIET*

A DELL TRADE PAPERBACK

CLUTTER
CONTROL

Jeff Campbell
of
The Clean Team

A DELL TRADE PAPERBACK

Published by
Dell Publishing
a division of
Bantam Doubleday Dell Publishing Group, Inc.
666 Fifth Avenue
New York, New York 10103

ISBN: 0-440-50339-6

Printed in the United States of America

Published simultaneously in Canada

May 1992

10   9   8   7   6   5

SEM

ACKNOWLEDGMENTS

Bill Redican helped write and rewrite this project. He also called upon his educational roots as a Ph.D. research psychologist to illuminate us on the psychology of clutter in Chapter 2. Thank you—again.

Charlene Richter, president of Getting Organized, in San Francisco, was kind enough to share her expert knowledge of clutter-bashing tactics both in person and through her Learning Annex class. She also works as an individual clutter consultant, in case you're looking for a good one. And we are grateful to Pat Shark of Contain Wares, Costa Mesa, California, for her patient advice on shelving systems. Thank you both.

Mike Curry, Sean Hyland, and my other friends and partners at The Clean Team kept things going even after a fire on St. Patrick's Day destroyed our office building. You all did what you had to do, and then you did some more. Thank you.

In memory of Wally and Ann.

Contents

CLUTTER
CONTROL

INTRODUCTION

Ask a dozen people what drives them crazy around their house—besides their spouse, of course—and chances are most will mention clutter high on the list. If it's not a universal irritant, it's surely an all-American one.

The consequences of clutter are lamentably too familiar:

- You can't find things, and you waste time looking for them, over and over again.
- Any sense of beauty or order in a room is out of the question.
- You're continually stymied trying to complete simple daily tasks.
- You can't even begin to clean the house.
- Your living space is uncomfortable and depressing.
- You're surrounded by evidence of what a colossal failure at housekeeping you appear to be.
- The house is too much of a mess to have company visit, and when they do "pop over," it's humiliating.
- You're perpetually living in the past, and never have a sense of catching up with the present.
- Certain accumulations in your home can be a fire hazard or even a health hazard.

It's pretty clear that clutter is the bane of many existences. But what is the nature of this beast? The root of the word *clutter* is Middle English *clot*—a lump. Just as a blood clot stops the flow of vitality in the body, so household clutter blocks the proper flow of a home.

To us, clutter appears to involve one or both of two undesirable events: One of them is related to things. You have too much stuff, and/or the stuff you have is in a state of chaos. As we become a more affluent and object-oriented culture, the accumulation of more and better stuff is a phenomenon that has become a way of life. It's difficult to limit and organize this accumulation. The other undesirable event is related to time: interruptions of it, not enough of it, and not knowing where to start.

To some people, household clutter is all those things that get in the way—especially when trying to clean or organize, or to prepare for a visitor. To others, clutter is the relentlessly growing mountains of paper in their house—bills, mail, magazines, newspapers, recipes, invoices, receipts, notes, lists, and scraps of paper that accumulate faster than they can be read, filed, paid, given away, or discarded. For other people, clutter is mostly an organizational problem—the *lack* of a system for paying bills, keeping appointments, or arranging the closets or drawers so things can be successfully and painlessly retrieved once they've been put away. And for you it may be the closets filled to overflowing (but nothing ready to wear), or the packed bookshelves (but nothing new to read), or the garage (where it's nearly impossible to find anything or cram anything else into, let alone the car).

For many, what's annoying about clutter is the lost time caused by it—starting with the wasted time looking for misplaced things, but also including the cluttered feeling caused by too many things to do in the time available, and the clutter of interruptions when you finally find the time to try to get something done. Clutter even has a financial impact if you pay for storing stuff you never use, if you buy things you'll never need, if you end up buying more of something you already have an ample supply of—or if you come home from a tiring and time-consuming shopping trip without the most important item you went to the store to get in the first place.

No matter how we're personally afflicted by clutter, most of us already have some idea what to do about it. If you have too much stuff, it doesn't take a rocket scientist to figure out that you'll have to reduce the volume of it in some way. But even after you've gotten rid of as much as you're willing to, you've still got to organize what's left, or the mountain starts to grow again.

The idea is to take the germ of the solution that you already know, feed it, give it light and air, and let it bloom. That's one of the goals of this book—to give you confidence and encouragement—to move you to action so you put your hunches to work. Plus we'll fill in the gaps with some field-tested remedies—a team approach in which you'll get all the credit!

In the meantime, your stuff is driving you up the wall. You already know that having a garage sale would be a good idea. But not only haven't you had one, you still don't have the willpower to resist other people's garage sales. More stuff! Just what you need! And your house looks more and more like the flea markets you try to avoid. Even if you've managed to get everything in sight tucked away, do you know what's in your closets, cabinets, drawers, and garage? Heck, no!

Don't beat yourself up if you're a clutterer. You're not alone. And this situation isn't a lot different from trying to lose a few pounds. People who are overweight certainly know that it would be helpful to change their eating behavior and to exercise more. However, just being armed with these sterling facts does not make the pounds drop off in awe. The hard work is putting what you know into practice. That's why diet books are so popular. Many, many people would dearly love to find a system that makes losing weight easy and palatable: something—anything— that will take the work out of losing weight. Or that will deliver the willpower necessary for the undertaking. Or that will give us the encouragement we need. Or that will just teach us how to prepare food that tastes so good we'll hardly notice we're dieting.

Likewise with clutter. Getting rid of clutter is like putting your house on a diet. But just wanting to get rid of it won't make it happen. It can be painful to let go of our material goods. We may view them as a reflection of our lives and of our very impact while here on earth. They enhance our feelings of self-worth and security. They can represent our memories of family, loved ones, and days gone by.

So a big part of ourselves may not want any part of a household uncluttering project, thank you, despite the fact that the clutter is driving us crazy. At some level, uncluttering appears to be asking us to throw a chunk of ourselves away. Hence one of the reasons for an impasse over clutter: It torments us and we have a good idea of what to do about it, yet remedies appear to threaten some basic feelings about ourselves and our world. So we do nothing—but watch, helplessly, as the clutter, in blissful ignorance, piles higher and spreads wider.

What you're passing up by clinging to all this stuff are a number of substantial payoffs: a wonderful sense of freedom; an ability (and the time) to manage your daily life; a capacity to live more in the present; an appreciation of a more beautiful home environment; and a more productive life. Imagine how great it would be if you didn't have the feeling that your home is running you instead of the other way around. Imagine everything in your home being in its rightful place. Imagine that you could find something when you needed it—not after an

Our family was able to find its can opener in only twenty-five fun-packed minutes.

exasperating search or by accident a week later. Imagine that your filing system allowed you to schedule and keep your appointments, pay your bills in a timely fashion, and keep the flow of paper smooth. The liberating feelings of accomplishment and relief that come with banishing clutter are tangible, real, and healthy.

But you already knew that. And you're probably adult enough to know that life requires sensible compromises—among them ones that will enable you to shift from living the way you do now to living the way you would prefer.

Grand! You say you're quite prepared to compromise, to change some habits so you can get the clutter under control. There's one additional roadblock: inertia. We could all use encouragement to get the ball rolling, the necessary dose of willpower to take action. It's the same mind-set achieved just before starting a successful diet or exercise program. If you can see that there are direct and practical steps you can take to unclutter your home, and that you're far from being alone in this endeavor, you'll be more likely to feel that you can succeed.

Is there any wonder you're having such a hard time getting started? Besides all the motivational factors, you haven't been trained in organizing. Even if you took Home Economics, household organization probably wasn't taught during the course. How do you set about organizing a clothes closet, for example? What do you do first? If you're like many people, you don't even particularly want to be trained in organizing. You just want instant results (like an organized closet). And some direct answers. That's our job—to give you direct and practical answers to questions about how to unclutter and organize your household wherever it's bothering you.

How do you know that you have a household clutter problem? We're not going to give you one of those self-scoring tests that you're doomed to fail. But here are a few questions you might want to ask yourself in a benign manner.

- Do you save magazines indefinitely that may have articles you really "should" read because you might miss something?
- Do you need more than one "repair drawer" or "junk drawer"?
- Do you save things that seem just too good to throw away even though you have no particular plans for ever using them?
- Are you storing all sorts of things on behalf of your grown children?
- Do you save broken things for years, never repair them, and then realize you don't like or need them anyway?
- Do you lose your keys or wallet or purse regularly?
- Do you buy things you already have, but didn't know it because the cupboard is a rat's nest?
- Do you have under your kitchen sink cleaning products—including numerous "miracle" cleaners—that you've never touched?
- Do you save spare parts to unknown things?
- Do you collect empty boxes?
- Do you know what bills are coming due this week or this month?

- Have you lost a chunk of change because you're late with payments and get zapped with late charges and interest because there's no time to write the checks?
- Has your collection of porcelain ducks, frogs, penguins, elephants, etc., begun to seem like it's just something else to clean—without the interest or fun that it once had?
- Are some drawers or shelves stuffed so full that you can use only the items on top?
- Do you keep putting things in places that you know aren't right and then tell yourself you are just putting them there "for now"?
- Do you live in a house with more storage space than ever before, but every spare space fills up immediately and you still don't have enough?
- Do you feel guilty and depressed about the state of your home?
- Would you entertain more often (if at all) if you could only get things under control?

Aren't you glad that wasn't a test?

If you didn't feel that you had an interest in controlling clutter, it's doubtful you would have picked up and read this far. So let's move on to parts of this book that are more like answers than reminders of our lack of organizational success.

Here's how we've organized this book. As we did in our two previous books on cleaning (*Speed Cleaning* for weekly cleaning and *Spring Cleaning* for the big jobs), first we propose a set of rules that can apply to all manner of households, regardless of their size, number of occupants, or magnitude of clutter.

After the rules, we explore some of the psychological roots of the clutter problem, because at heart it's a behavioral phenomenon. Insight into the dynamics of your cluttering behavior may afford you great and tangible relief.

In the next and largest part of the book, we list specific, step-by-step solutions to clutter and organization problems. Not hints at solutions. Solutions. We call it "Uncluttering Guides: An Alphabetical List." For each topic we will tell you what items (if any) you'll need to implement a solution and how to proceed each step of the way until you've solved a specific clutter problem. But our approach is practical. It's usually how to do something, not what sort of organizing gadget to run out and buy: We want you to put your house on a diet, not stuff it into a girdle.

As in our preceding books on cleaning, we're not suggesting that there are no other alternatives. There are. But the solutions we offer have been tested by us or by others and found to solve specific clutter problems. We don't list four or five different solutions. We prefer to do the research, test the options, and then offer you the best solution available. We confess that this is just a touch authoritarian, but it's exactly the approach that will save you the most time.

In "Uncluttering Guides," where you jump in is up to you. Topics are in alphabetical order. If you want to implement them all, just start at the beginning. Or rate them in order of what is driving you crazy the most and start there.

Chapter 1

THE UNCLUTTERING RULES

Here are the rules that are your path out of a life-style bogged down with stuff, immobilized by disorganization, and stymied by interruption. They will assist you in your day-to-day decision-making process when clutter or household organization is the subject at hand. Keep these rules in ongoing use even after you've uncluttered your life, so you'll keep it that way.

RULE 1
When in doubt, throw it out.

Absolutely nothing else we say in this book can have such a liberating effect on your life. We like testimonials, and here's one quoted in its entirety from a "Dear Abby" column (*San Francisco Chronicle*, March 11, 1991):

> **DEAR ABBY:** I related to the letter about the husband who was a pack rat because I'm one, too. After years of bachelorhood, I

married a woman who'd throw out the newspaper while I was still reading it.

In the fourth year of our marriage I was sent overseas, leaving my wife, who was pregnant. When I completed the tour, I was reassigned to the Pentagon, and my wife had the thankless task of selling our home and packing and moving us to the Washington, D.C., area. She handled all of this like a real pro.

A year later we were entertaining guests, and I told the story of our move, bragging about how well my wife had handled everything alone. She casually remarked, "Yes, and it gave me the opportunity to throw out all the junk Bill had been carrying around all these years." I was shocked to hear her say this, as she'd never mentioned it before, so I asked, "And just what did you throw out?" She calmly replied, "What are you missing?" Try as I did, I couldn't identify a single item I missed. Then she said, "You tell me what you're missing, and I'll tell you whether or not I threw it out."

Everyone (including me) had a good laugh at my expense, but it certainly proved her point.

So, all you pack rats, clean out your closets and drawers, put the junk in boxes, then take the whole lot to one of those storage lockers. After paying the storage bill for several years, you will be amazed at how much you can live without.

—BEEN THERE AND LEARNED

DEAR BEEN THERE: As incredible as it may seem, public auctions are held to sell furniture, clothing, furs and valuable jewelry that were in storage for many years and never claimed. The owners either couldn't pay the storage bill, or they died having forgotten that their property had been stored.

—ABBY

It's encouraging to read about someone who has seen the light at the end of the (cluttered) tunnel. We would have advised him to skip the step about paying for a storage locker for a few years. Besides saving the money, he wouldn't have to drag all the stuff back home again to have a garage sale.

There's an abundance of opportunities to acquire things in our lives. We are invited to do so by every imaginable source of advertisement; by our perpetual comparisons of our possessions with those of our friends, relatives, and neighbors; and by our own private insecurities and habits. We feel like we're building our nest. The more things we can add to our nest, the more secure and successful we feel.

Once an item makes it into our nest, a metamorphosis takes place as it becomes "ours," and its value is completely transformed. For example, before a crystal decanter becomes our possession, if it should be broken or lost it would barely qualify as an accident. Once we get it into our home, however, if it is broken we regard it as a disaster. Obviously this has something to do with how much we paid for it, but it can acquire its own almost inexplicable value, which involves much more than money alone.

Trouble is, acquiring everything you have the chance to is just not worth it. The price paid is a lifetime of being loaded down by things we wouldn't miss if they were taken away from us: things we couldn't find if we needed them, things we don't even remember we have unless we see them, unused things that ultimately crowd out the necessary things we actually use. Don't wait for that to happen—do it of your own free will now.

The Cost of Storing Your Things

One major incentive to declutter is the expense of maintaining all that stuff. You'll be amazed when you figure out the actual cost of keeping it. First calculate how much you're paying for each square foot of your home by dividing the square footage by the monthly rent or mortgage. For example, if you live in a 1,500-square-foot house and have a $1,500 monthly payment, that's obviously $1 per square foot per month. Now multiply by how many square feet are devoted to storage. This can be an eye-opening experience. Let's say you've let an entire room slowly drift into a "junk" room even though it was originally intended as a guest bedroom or a sewing room. You've got 100 square feet or more devoted to storage in that one room alone. So you're paying 100 × $1

= $100 a month for the privilege of having a junk room. That might be worth it if you were storing prized and valuable possessions.

Unfortunately, this monthly $100 bill is for storing items you don't even look at—unless you take a peek when you open the door to toss something else in the collection. Worse yet, just knowing what lurks behind that door nags you silently. You also have a crisis if you do have a guest. And your sewing plans are on indefinite hold—like perhaps for this lifetime.

A "junk" room is only the most obvious place to look. For many homes, it's just the tip of the iceberg. Consider some of the other fertile places around the house to discover caches of junk. And add their cost to the first figure you came up with. For example:

• How many square feet of each closet in your home are used to store things you don't use? It's not nice to remind you of all the clothes in those closets that no longer fit. Let's just say they're too large, shall we, and leave it at that. Or maybe you don't wear them because they've gone out of style. With luck, they'll come back in style in thirty years, but do you think you'll actually wear those musty antiques?

• What about under the beds? Gifts you've received that you're never going to use. Perfectly fine other things that are "too good to throw away." Broken things.

• Look in drawers, but don't count the things you use every day—or even once a year. What about the linen from your grandmother for a table that wouldn't even fit into your dining room? Linen with spots, linen with holes, linen you're saving for your kids. (They don't even like the brand-new things you get them for their birthday and Christmas. Lord knows what they'll want with things you don't even know what to do with.) And then there are the drawers bursting with unused blouses, T-shirts, socks, underwear, incomplete bed sheet sets, worn-out towels, photographs, calendars, college papers, postcards, ancient mail, maps, newspapers, matchbooks, and mystery items.

• Bookshelves filled with books you haven't looked at in years—if ever. Or with porcelain frogs. Or with liquor decanters. We're not opposed to collections per se; it's just that it's sometimes difficult to appreciate the beauty of a porcelain frog if there are thirty-seven of them.

• Don't forget books that are stored in places other than bookshelves, including unloved cookbooks, outgrown children's books, and unused reference books.

• Appliances and gadgets you never use. They're often in the kitchen drawers and cabinets, but don't forget the extra set of speakers or the foot massager, no matter where you have them stashed.

• The freezer. You have things in there that no one in the house knows about or can identify anymore—let alone would be willing to eat.

• The garage, carport, basement, or attic—junk heaven. Tires to cars you no longer own. Athletic equipment such as the exercise bike that started in the living room, migrated to the bedroom, and is now relegated to dusty solitude. Dead clothes that no longer fit in your bulging closets. Bed parts. Derelict lawn furniture or equipment. Pieces of lumber left over from a project half completed in 1976. If by chance you can no longer fit your car or cars into your garage or carport, don't forget to add the additional depreciation caused by storing it outside. And add the square footage of the garage to your total storage bill.

The point: You have junk stored in many places in your home, and it costs you real money to store it.

Here are some guidelines for deciding what should be tossed and what should be kept. (When we say "tossed," we are including giving it away or selling it, of course.)

Popular Excuses for Keeping Things Forever

BEFORE

AFTER

If you aren't actually using something, why allow it to complicate your home? I have a section of my desk drawer that is reserved just for pens. It's always overflowing. The problem is, if my favorite pen isn't there, I will turn the house upside down looking for it rather than use any of the pens that are stuffed into this drawer. Solution? Save the favorite pen plus three or four spares and toss the rest. Now there's room for adding something to the drawer should the occasion arise. And the drawer even closes easily, for the first time in years. If you have several pairs of eyeglasses with outdated prescriptions, give them away. (Several charities solicit them.) It's different if you use something occasionally. (Christmas ornaments are a good example.)

Give your grown kids' things back to them. If you do, maybe they'll learn to deal with clutter a couple of decades earlier than you did. The same goes for your friends, neighbors, or other relatives for whom you are storing things.

Please don't try the old excuse "It's too nice to throw away." Especially if it's so nice, give it to someone who will use it and appreciate it.

It it's broken, fix it or toss it. If it's ripped, have it mended. If it doesn't fit, have it altered. Don't put it anywhere just "for now" and keep it in a perpetual holding pattern.

If you find a screw or have one left over after a project, don't start saving them. It will drive you crazy. Usually when you buy something that needs a screw, it will have one included. If it doesn't, you can get the exact number of appropriate screws while you're at the store. That's much faster and easier than picking through all your saved screws (which over time have a way of starting to get nails mixed in with them, plus a few tacks, push-pins, washers, picture hangers, and other small, sharp, and rusty objects). And even if you do search your collection and ultimately find three of the screws you need, the project will probably call for four of them.

Since most households do have need of a nail or a screw occasionally, just remember that almost any method of acquiring and storing them is preferable to the one-at-a-time-whenever-you-happen-upon-one method and then adding it to the little box or mayonnaise jar full of them.

Save the stereo box for thirty days. If the stereo hasn't broken by then, discard the box. (If you bought it by mail order, save it for the full warranty period.) Unless you're planning on moving (have the date set, etc.), don't keep the box "because you'll need it when you move." That's true, but it may be years away. You or the moving company can use another box when the time comes.

Rule 1 still counts if you don't know what an item is. My mother will save something even though she's not at all sure what it is. She'll convince herself that it fell out of her refrigerator or something else vital and that if she throws it away, she will only then discover where it should have gone. If she weren't my mother, I would point out to her that she has lived for over sixty years. If she hasn't learned what something is by now, there is no particular likelihood she will do so in the next sixty years.

RULE 2
Use it or lose it.

This rule is particularly helpful when you are attempting to implement Rule 1 and are getting rid of some of your stuff. How do you decide what to keep and what to toss? Sensible advice for this rule is if you're not using something, get rid of it. This does not allow you to plan on using it tomorrow. How does the song go? "*Mañana* never comes."

Future time is especially not a factor in this rule. "Use it" refers to the here and now. It doesn't mean some time in the future. You don't have to use something every day, but you can't use the excuse that it "might come in handy after the earthquake"—unless it's a flashlight or something sensible. Not your collection of lampshades. If you haven't put up any strawberry preserves since 1962, despite your strong conviction that you will do so again next year, you can safely give away your mason jars and lids.

There is a twist to applying this rule that's very helpful to parents trying to teach children about clutter. You might phrase the rule: "Put it away or lose it." We received a letter from a woman who told us how well this version of the rule worked for her. She cleaned every Saturday morning and just threw out anything left in her way! It didn't matter if it was clothes, toys, or food. Out it went. No bluffing. A particularly brief period of time elapsed before the house was *completely* picked up by early Saturday morning. Hard to argue with success.

According to our mail, the biggest roadblock many people had in implementing our first book, *Speed Cleaning,* in their home was that the house was too cluttered for them even to start. Rule 2 is a solution to that problem and more: You reduce clutter, *and* you make housecleaning that much easier.

RULE 3

Efficiency counts, so store things accordingly.

Perhaps you've seen the classic movie *Cheaper by the Dozen*. The head of the household in this movie was an efficiency expert. (Remember them? Businesses used to hire them all the time. They still do, but they call them management engineers or industrial engineers now.) This particular efficiency expert devoted his life to the study of such things. He found, for example, that it was considerably faster to button his shirt starting at the top and buttoning downward compared to starting at the bottom and buttoning upward. This little gem of knowledge in itself may not reduce clutter, but efficiency boils down to a maximum of output with a minimum of input, and it's a concept that's crucial to managing clutter.

Efficient storage reduces clutter by making it easier to replace things after each use. If it's easier it's more likely to happen. Efficient storage means that what you need is close to where you use it or where you expect it to be. Move things so they are efficiently placed for use and replacement. For example, if the recycling bins are in the far end of the garage, no one is going to use them. In the kitchen, move the silverware and plates to a drawer and cupboard between the table and the dishwasher. Put the glasses between the sink and the dishwasher. Since the kids normally throw their coats just inside the door (if you're lucky), move the coatrack there, even though it looks better next to the desk down the hall. It's not carved in stone that you must store the vacuum in the upstairs closet. Move it downstairs, where it's more convenient. If your excuse is that there is no room in the downstairs closet, see the section on how to clean it out, get it organized, and create the room you need (page 64).

Efficient storage also means that things you use most often are stored in the most easily accessible places. In other words, "hot" items go in "hot" places. You'll have your own list of "hot" items, of course, but it'll probably include things such as measuring spoons and cups, keys, bottles of spray cleaners, the roll of cellophane tape, the corkscrew, the good pair of scissors, the dishwashing soap, etc. Resist the temptation to return rarely used items to a "hot" (and therefore convenient) spot. If you're not alert, the anchovy paste will end up in front of the mustard. The pewter polish will get shoved in front of the powdered cleanser. Or the wood bleach will block your access to the furniture polish. "Hot" places are easily reachable ones such as top drawers, eye-level cupboard shelves, and the front sections of shelves.

Store all similar things together—such as all the different sizes and shapes of flower vases you own. When you need one, you only have to look in one place. Also, you'll have no decision to make after you clean a vase and wonder where to put it. The same applies to food inside the cupboards and even inside the fridge. The easier you make it for things to get put where they belong, the less clutter will appear. You'll also have a fighting chance of finding what you're looking for if it's where it belongs. That can be a surprisingly gratifying experience.

RULE 4

Handle some things once.

This rule is necessary because of the excuse "for now." For example, "I will put this jacket here for now," or "I will put this stack of papers here for now." This phrase should be forbidden to a known clutterer.

Once you say "for now," you are admitting that you are going to

"FOR NOW"

handle whatever it is more than once. That seemingly innocuous decision increases clutter and at least doubles your work load. What you're really doing when you utter those forbidden words is putting off making a decision about it right then and there. Don't be lazy. That decision won't go away just because you put if off, and it won't be any easier to make later on. So make your decisions about things right then and there.

Here's one way to apply this rule: When mail arrives, don't just idly sort through it looking for something interesting. Instead, stand next to a recycling bin or trash can as you sort. Toss the appropriate pieces then and there. It's a very liberating thing to do. Put bills in the "Bills" file of your file cabinet (see Rule 7). Put interesting catalogs or ads with the newspaper and look at them after you read the paper. Then file them as needed or recycle them with the newspaper.

We met a woman who stood at the trash can as her kids brought home paperwork from school. She looked at each paper, made the appropriate comments directly to her kids, and tossed it into the trash. If the paper was special in some way and merited saving, she had a place for it in her filing cabinet.

My mother's repair drawer was a great example of the lengths to which the "for now" philosophy could be carried. Putting something in that drawer was exactly the same as throwing it away, because *nothing* ever emerged from it. We just kept more and bigger repair drawers to hold all that stuff.

When the opportunity arises, or whenever you feel the words "for now" starting to form on your lips, remind yourself to handle the item once. Don't leave it in some temporary holding area instead of where it ultimately belongs.

RULE 5
Recycle it.

We're not talking about just paper, aluminum, glass, and plastic. You may argue that you throw these items away anyway, so how does recycling help with uncluttering? Well, for one thing, it's a good habit to get used to putting certain things in certain places. In addition, many people have a tough time parting with containers, especially glass bottles. Mayonnaise jars are good for storing bacon fat, and pickle jars or peanut-butter jars are just right for something else. Reycling finally allows the world's bottle-savers to put their bottles to good use. Recycle them. The same goes for plastic Cool Whip containers, with their irresistible resealing lid, and microwave plates that remain after the dinner has been eaten. Even if you can't recycle plastic in your area, don't save these disposable items.

Other things can be recycled also. What about clothes you no longer wear or fit into? Recycle them into the hands of someone who needs them. Don't forget old sweaters and shoes that aren't so obvious when you open the closet door. What about books that overflow the capacity of your bookshelves? Sell them to a used-books store, or give them to a school library. Magazines can be given to a school or hospital or nursing home full of folks who will enjoy them. If you don't want to go to the trouble of finding a new home for your old magazines, recycle them with your newspapers if allowed. Old towels can be used for rags only if you need more rags. Otherwise, recycle them along with your old clothes. The same goes for unused linen, baby clothes, diapers, ties, belts, purses, wallets, plants, or bikes. In fact, almost any inanimate object in your house is a candidate for reuse by someone else.

RULE 6
Pick a number and stick with it.

If you really do use an empty mayonnaise jar for storing fat drippings, go ahead and save one. But if you use one mayonnaise jar every six months for drippings, and you purchase mayonnaise approximately once a month for consumption, you only need to save one jar to have a sufficient supply. One. *Uno.* One more than zero. Don't save any more jars until you use the one you've saved.

If you intend on saving boxes for packaging future gifts, pick a number and stick with it. If you're convinced that you must save a box for each of the different potential sizes of gifts, you really ought to call a spade a spade and just open a store, because that's what you'll have with so many boxes. Limit your collection to four boxes of varying sizes stored inside the largest one. That should be all you'll ever need at any one time, or at least until you have a chance to replenish your supply. When you reach your number, don't save another box until you use one from your supply. If you do come across another irresistible box, then toss one when you add the new one to your collection.

Whatever you do, don't exceed the chosen number. It's not fair to change the number willy-nilly. Pick a number for other things around the house that contribute to overall clutter. For example, decide to keep two weeks' worth of *Newsweek* or *Time*. Each week, throw away the issue that's three weeks old when the new one arrives.

If you have a passion for purchasing, this rule is for you. Purses are prime examples. Once again, pick a sensible number of purses to keep, and stick with it. If you decide on seven, this means that the other purses are clutter. Rank your top seven purses, give the others to charity, and don't buy a new one until you're willing to let one go.

Use this rule with shoes, socks, porcelain frogs, mustards in the fridge, or packages of paper towels in the cupboard. Also work clothes. Two sets are enough. Any more than that and you're just trying to get around giving away your old clothes. Junk drawer? Yes, you can keep it, but only one per household—not one per person or one per room.

Instead of a number, you can use a capacity if it's appropriate. For example, when you've accumulated more books than will fit into your bookshelves, it's time to get rid of some books.

RULE 7

Use a file cabinet.

We feel as strongly about this as Hoover felt about a chicken in every pot. Every contemporary home needs a file cabinet—not just those with a home office or those belonging to your superorganized friends. Even if you don't have a desk—or instead of one if you don't have room—invest in a file cabinet. You can always use the dining room table as a temporary desk, but nothing else in the house is a substitute for a file cabinet.

File cabinets start at about $40 for an inexpensive one with two drawers. An office-quality file cabinet of the same size can be two or three times as much. There are definite advantages to the more expensive ones: the drawers open fully so you can easily file all the way to the back. The drawers in the cheap ones don't open more than two-thirds of the way, so filing in the back of the drawer is always a pain. The more expensive ones have more reliable, stronger, and quieter opening and closing mechanisms. But even if you get the cheapest one available, it's still a great deal.

The two-drawer letter-size model is the right size for most homes. We will list some of the items to store in your cabinet below, which will help you decide if you need more than two drawers. You will find an Uncluttering Guide on page 86 on setting up your new filing system.

Some new cabinets have built-in metal frames for hanging file folders. If not, purchase an add-on frame for each drawer. And get a supply of the hanging files themselves. One of the reasons some people don't like file cabinets is because they have never used them with hanging files. These hanging files are what changed the cabinet into the wonderful clutter-buster it is.

Besides being a perfect storage place for such obvious choices as bills, important papers, and correspondence, the file cabinet is just right for warranty cards, product information, instruction booklets, stationery, photos, stamps, your kids' important schoolwork, report cards, spare batteries, diskettes, pens, pencils, tax returns, receipts, invoices, telephone books, and certain other books you want nearby, such as dictionaries, catalogs, address books, photo albums, and more. All sorts of nontraditional items can be stored in files, to your advantage.

RULE 8
Do something.

This rule really isn't as flip as it sounds. We're encouraging you to proceed to action in order to solve or fix something that's bothering you. In the Introduction, we suggested that most of us have some idea of what to do to solve our own clutter problems. We may not know exactly what to do, or exactly where to start, or what to toss and what to save, or what we need to buy in the way of shelves or storage baskets. But we do know we need to clean out, toss, and organize. Unfortunately, for many of us, what we do best with our clutter is to fret about it and mull it over. We may practically salivate when we see a catalog with a section of products for getting organized or when we see a sale on closet organizers, but we're still stuck by our own indecision and inertia.

In fact, much of the thinking we do about clutter can lead directly to inaction. The more you think about something and become aware of the possible solutions, ramifications, and roadblocks to those solutions, the more you're racked with indecision and inaction.

Embrace your own little imperfections. Even if you live to be a hundred, you'll never be as organized as your friend John, but then again you'll never be as messy as your friend Deborah, either. Get the areas of clutter that bother you under control and quit beating yourself up over the rest. Even if what you do is unsuccessful, you'll feel better. Besides, it's quite unlikely your efforts will make the problem worse— particularly if you use these rules and the Uncluttering Guides that follow to solve specific headaches.

RULE 9

A place for everything, and everything in its place.

Obviously your parents thought of this rule before we did, but maybe that's just another reason why it's so important for getting rid of clutter. Some clutter is just stuff that belongs someplace else. Whether it's the kids' toys strewn through the house, a closet full of clothes that no one in the family wears any longer, newspapers piled in the corner, or paper stacked on the desk, these items are clutter as long as they're not in their proper place.

Clearly, it's much easier to decide to put everything in its place than it is actually to do it—especially if you're fresh out of places. Several of the earlier rules will help you reduce the number of things in your household. The Uncluttering Guides that follow will help you increase the number of places for all your things.

The flip side of this rule means that if everything is in its place, you can find an item precisely when you want it. That event in and of itself can sometimes make your day.

RULE 10

Items displayed in the house have to pass a test.

This seems only fair. After all, you have only so much space. The items taking up that space should justify themselves. It's not a complicated test. They just have to have a valid reason for being there. The reason can involve function *or* form. For example, if the antique clock on the coffee table no longer works, it has lost its function. But it may still be quite beautiful to you and therefore has an attractive form. No problem. It passes the test. But it doesn't pass just because someone put it there "for now" five years ago and it's never been moved since, or because someone gave it to you who might notice if it's gone, or because you don't know where else to put it.

The way to implement this rule is to walk through each room of your house and quickly test each item displayed on buffets, end tables, coffee tables, nightstands, counters, mantels, shelves, or anywhere else. Examine each item as you come to it. Ask questions such as: Why am I keeping it? What is it doing there? If it has a function, does it work? Am I sick and tired of dusting or cleaning it? Do I have others like it stored elsewhere? For the form side of the test, ask if you enjoy seeing it as you enter the room. How does this item really look sitting there for all the world to see or to use? Use your critical eye.

Don't rid your home of things you cherish. But you will likely discover that many of the knickknacks, trinkets, and bric-a-brac sitting around your home fail the test. All the better. Anything that fails is one less thing to dust. Remove such items and deal with them accordingly: discard, sell, give away, or store elsewhere.

If you're not sure what to do with items that didn't pass the test (such as the ashtrays made by one of your children), try putting them away in storage areas for a test period of one month. Your guilt is assuaged, and you've made progress in clutter control. Who knows what will happen in a month? We have an inkling you'll have forgotten about them completely—unless it's to remember, when you're cleaning, that you have fewer things to dust or wipe. When you clean out the drawers or closets they're temporarily stored in, you can make further decisions about them as needed.

RULE 11
Don't do things "later."

Let's say you just spent an hour picking up in the family room. It's in impeccable shape—splendidly uncluttered by things that don't belong there. You know only too well that it can be turned into a war zone by the family in minutes: discarded clothes, food, dirty dishes, shoes, toys (kids', dogs', and cats'), soft drink and/or beer cans, dirty ashtrays, school papers, newspapers, magazines, cups, and glasses.

It goes something like this: One child comes into the family room with a soda and turns on the TV. He tosses his coat on a chair and rummages around for *TV Guide*. The desire for a sandwich becomes irresistible. He abandons the empty soda can and returns to the kitchen, gliding by both the recycling bins where the soda can belongs as well as the coatrack where the jacket belongs. A few more trips by other family members and the room is done for.

THINGS NOT TO DO LATER: A PARTIAL LIST

1. If you brought stuff into a room, take it back out *the very next time you leave that room* (after you're done with it, of course).
2. Take things upstairs if you are going there anyway.
3. Take things downstairs if you are going there anyway.
4. Take everything out of the car that was added this trip.
5. Pick up things when they drop.
6. Wipe up spills when they happen.
7. Vacuum up messes when they occur.
8. Wash dirty dishes and wipe off the counters before the food dries on them.
9. Fold the clothes when they emerge from the dryer.
10. Iron clothes while they're still slightly damp.

A lot of the clutter in your home will disappear if you follow this rule. It's not much more than leaving a room the way you found it. If there wasn't toothpaste spread on the sink before you came into the room, there shouldn't be any there when you leave it. This rule solves clutter problems without adding one second of time or one ounce of work to anyone's overwhelmed schedule. It doesn't involve any extra time to take dirty dishes to the kitchen if you're going there anyway to get a glass of water. It doesn't take any extra time to carry your shoes to your bedroom if you're going up there anyway to do your homework.

In some cases it actually saves a bunch of time. If you don't wipe up a spill when it happens, it will eventually take much more than a simple wipe. It may call for hard scrubbing or several different scrapers or cleaners that require a trip to the garage or the store. It may even have developed into a permanent stain.

Naturally, you know and practice all these sterling principles. It's the other members of your family who are somewhat less enlightened. So how do you get them to cooperate? Setting an example sometimes works (every ice age or so).

But this rule isn't going to get off the ground unless everyone practices it, and consistently so. Try calling the household together and sitting down at a peace conference with them. Tell them the subject of the meeting, and all parties will probably readily agree (with varying degrees of enthusiasm, perhaps) that clutter is a problem. Ask everyone to volunteer ideas for your own "things not to do later" list. Don't allow accusations to be hurled. Just make the list. Read them our list if you need help getting started with yours. Next, make a contract, with your new list as its terms. All parties must affirm that they agree to the terms. Then agree on a list of rewards for adhering to the contract and punishments for infringing it. Nothing extravagant or gruesome. Just an appealing payoff for compliance and a somewhat obnoxious deterrent for noncompliance.

There are several additional ideas for things to do daily that will help keep the house civilized between cleanings, save time when you do clean, and contribute to your sense of successfully managing your home.

In the bathroom: Put a window squeegee (or a squeegee specially designed for the bathroom) in your shower. The last person to shower should use the squeegee to remove water from the walls and doors that would otherwise dry and turn into difficult-to-remove water spots. It only takes a minute or so. Not only will this make cleaning the shower easier than it's ever been before, the shower also will continue to look clean for a much longer time. If you have particularly hard water in your area, take one more step and quickly wipe the walls dry with a towel after you've squeegeed them. Now cleaning the shower every week or every other week practically drops off your list of things to do because it never really stays dirty. Do the same thing around the sink. The last user should sop up the water on the counter and then dry and shine the chrome. Dry the sink itself if hard water also makes that difficult to clean later. Use a towel that's on its way to be laundered, or leave a special towel or cleaning cloth hanging nearby.

In the kitchen: Wipe the counter, sink, and chrome dry after each meal. Also after preparing a meal, take a couple of dampened paper towels and wipe the floor—but only the small area of the floor close to where you prepared the food—and in front of the refrigerator, if it needs it.

For the rest of the house: Vacuum as often as daily when pet hairs or general debris are getting to you. We're not suggesting a full-blown vacuuming, just a quick vacuuming of the main traffic areas for three or four minutes. To make this even faster, leave your vacuum in the corner of the dining room (or somewhere else, but not put away) during those times of the year that require frequent vacuuming. Besides making the house look so much better, this extra vacuuming also saves time when you do your regular cleaning. Your carpets and floors will look better longer and last longer.

RULE 12
Label things.

We're not talking about putting a label just on the kids' gym shorts, although that's a prudent idea. We're talking about labeling things around the house—things that people don't label because they don't think of it or because they think it isn't necessary. How often have you gone to a storage closet to retrieve something from a cardboard box you had stored there yourself, only to find that there are now six cardboard boxes there and they all look the same? You start by muscling down what you think is the correct box and taking off the tape with which you so carefully sealed it. After you discover that the item isn't in that box, you halfway reseal it with the used tape and start in on the next box. Let's say you do eventually find the item you're looking for—it's just that it's forty-five minutes and six boxes later. That's the kind of problem that labeling can avoid.

LABEL STORAGE BOXES

Label *all* storage boxes to avoid the grief outlined above. Get a good marking pen and, at least on cardboard boxes, write on the box itself. Try hard to avoid the label "Miscellaneous." Other examples of labels that may come back to haunt you are "Garage Sale" or "Charity." Even if your label ends up listing everything in the box, doing so is still simpler than looking through your entire collection of boxes. Usually you can get away with a label such as "Books" or "Summer Clothes"— as long as you don't have more than one box with that same label. Use a label just complete enough so you can tell what's in the box without actually opening it. When you add or remove items from a box, change the label accordingly.

LABEL FROZEN FOOD

Everything starts to look alike after a few days in the freezer. That's understandable if you wrap items in aluminum foil, of course, but food stored even in plastic wrap turns white and crystalline and becomes disguised quickly enough.

Put a roll of inch-wide masking tape and a pen in a drawer next to the freezer wrap of your choice. Use a length of the tape to make a label for everything you freeze. Also add the date to the label: If you have more than one package of chicken, you'll know which one to use first. As long as you have your tape handy, you might as well date even prepackaged frozen food so you'll know what to use first, what to save, and what to toss out when you defrost the freezer.

LABEL CUPBOARDS SOMETIMES

Labels on the inside of cupboard doors can help keep your cupboards from disintegrating into chaos about as fast as you can get them organized. Even with the best of intentions, when you or others in the household bring home the groceries and unload them into the cupboards, you can't exactly remember where you decided to put certain items. Putting labels on the inside of the cupboard doors will help prevent haphazard storage. You may need labels just until you and the family get used to putting certain things in certain places. But even if labels become a permanent installation, they can keep a major reorganization effort intact.

With small kids you can put the labels on the outside of the cupboards—especially the ones they tend to get into while looking for cereal, sugar, cookies, jam, peanut butter, bread, etc. Lord knows it's not that they need to know where these things are. Rather, it's a reminder of where to replace things when the users are finished with them. If they're too young for verbal labels, use pictures instead.

Speaking of your wonderful progeny, use labels generously in their rooms to teach them to put things where they belong. In the Uncluttering Guides that follow, see "Children's Rooms" on page 62 for more ideas.

RULE 13
Call in a professional.

A whole new profession has arisen of saintly people who make their living solving other people's clutter and organizational problems. They will come into your home and—working either with you or by themselves—will clean out the closets, install the necessary organizers, set up a filing system for you, and generally encourage the calm you've longed for to emerge from the chaos that's been driving you crazy.

How do you find a pro? Look in the yellow pages under "Organizing." In the San Francisco yellow pages they're listed under "Organizing Services and Systems—Household and Business." Another place to look is through community-oriented classes. Household organizing or anticlutter classes are taught several times a year in San Francisco, and the instructors usually work in the field themselves.

There's a catch to this rule, however: We insist that you use it only if you promise to follow all the other rules once the professional has come and gone. He or she will leave, and the clutter will return almost immediately unless you modify your behavior. Implementing this rule does not reduce the number of rules to just this one, in other words.

Chapter 2

THE PSYCHOLOGY OF CLUTTER

The landscape of your house matches the inner landscape of your thoughts and feelings. In other words, we can gain some insight into its nature by examining it from a psychological point of view. In all but the rarest of cases, it's not a medical problem. And (we hope) the need to clutter isn't programmed into us genetically: Chimpanzees make nests to sleep in, but they walk away from them after each use. And they do not have charming collections of coconuts, bugs, leaves, etc.

Just because it has psychological dimensions does not mean that anyone living amid a patch or two of clutter has a psychological problem. Were that true, we'd all be on the couch.

When Has Clutter Become Clutteritis?

Okay, at what point can we say that clutter has gone beyond the point of reasonableness? Where is the psychological boundary between a reasonable amount of clutter and a more persistent problem?

In our view, clutter becomes a problem that calls for action when one or more of the following situations arise for you or for other members of the household:

- It is creating feelings of depression, anxiety, or desperation.
- The need for more or better or newer stuff seems insatiable.
- You feel like you are not the master of your own life anymore: It feels like you're being controlled by your possessions.
- The disorder of your living space prevents you from feeling comfortable or creative or happy when you're there.
- You deride yourself for not being more organized.
- You're in chronic conflict with other household members over this issue.
- You're ashamed to have friends and relatives over to the house because it's such a mess, and you're feeling more and more isolated or eccentric as a result.

Those are some of the psychological landmarks indicating that clutter has passed beyond the point where it can be ignored—at least if you want to promote a happy and productive life. Now let's dig into some of the psychological needs that feed the clutter habit.

Too Much Stuff: Pack Rats

It's encouraging to see that psychologists are studying something as practical as the pack-rat personality. For example, psychology Professor Lynda W. Warren of California State University, San Bernardino, estimates that at least one person in ten in the United States is a chronic saver.[1] The most common excuses given by the two hundred pack rats she interviewed were:

1. "I might need it someday."
2. "They don't make them like this anymore."
3. "It reminds me of someone I love or someplace I've been."

I MIGHT NEED THEM SOMEDAY

Sound familiar, eh? We would like to propose the following rebuttals for each of these rationalizations:

1. Yes, you might need it someday. Then again, you might not. Assess the odds dispassionately. What will happen if you don't have the item on that imaginary day? Will you die? Will you be sick? Or will it just be an inconvenience that can be easily remedied? And are you going to save everything that you *might* need? If so, you'd have to live in a warehouse.

1. R. Lichtenstein, "The Pack-Rat Phenomenon," *San Francisco Examiner* (February 10, 1990), p. B-30.

2. No, they probaby don't make it like this anymore. But you can admire something without concluding that you have to own it. If you save everything that fits in this category, you'll need a second warehouse.

3. Yes, these things remind you of people and places. But they are only that—reminders. They are not the person or place in itself. The reality of the experience is still alive in you by virtue of the fact that you were forever changed by it. You are not betraying this person if you pass on an object that reminds you of him or her. (Can you imagine that person expecting you to be the object's custodian forever? What kind of friend is that?) If you fuss with the object, your affection can get displaced and fantasized so it focuses more on the object than the real human being it calls to mind. If you were to save a token of every meaningful experience, you'd better start looking for a third warehouse.

Of course, no one is proposing that you become completely unsentimental or ruthlessly Spartan. We are talking about motives that can run amok if they're hitched to objects that serve as symbols of security or attachments. The real roots of security and affection are within you.

The alternative is moderation. Take the middle path. Keep things that are genuinely important for your well-being. And keep things that you genuinely appreciate without feeling desperate or driven about keeping. And keep sentimental remembrances with a sense of joy, not obligation or guilt.

"This Is Me": The Roots of Clutter

The times in which we live will probably not be recorded as one of the great introspective or spiritual ages. Unfortunately, the safe money is on materialism—at least in the short term. Has any generation ever before had the abundance of material goods available to someone growing up in the West today? High-school graduates have their hopes set on a new BMW—not the beat-up Chevy their parents longed for after college. A prom calls for enough money to feed most Third World families for months and months.

What can account for such a phenomenal rise in the esteem of material goods? Look no farther than the sense of self, and the remarkable human ability to see the self represented or symbolized in objects. "See this collection of goodies? This is me—this is who I am. I am one swell person, as you can see."

So what's wrong with seeing oneself in an object? Doesn't everybody do it? Well, yes, they do. It is a supremely easy habit to fall into. But it has its problems. For one thing, on face value it is untrue. Our essence is not embodied in things. For another, the habit can lead to a frightful amount of offense being taken. "How dare you insult my collection of penguins! I won't ever speak to you again!" And we put our sense of self-worth out there on the line when we trot out our objects. If they are praised, we puff up and feel better. When they are scorned, we feel worse about ourselves. This can be quite a roller-coaster ride.

How do you get off the roller coaster? Don't cling to a fixed view of yourself—especially one that needs objects to keep it afloat. You're entitled to exist just as you are, without an array of psychological props through which you define yourself.

Look at the penniless ascetics of the world's ancient cultures: They have little more than a begging bowl and a sheet, and yet they can be radiant human beings. Here's a poem by the Japanese haiku poet Basho that says a lot in five lines:

> *My house*
> *Burnt down*
>
> *I own*
> *A better view*
>
> *Of the rising moon.*

There is also the story of the monk who used to burn his house down every few years to make sure he was not getting attached to material things. We are not advocating such strong measures; the much more moderate ones in this book will do just fine.

At some level of awareness, you become the caretaker for every scrap of stuff you keep. Don't kid yourself: You are devoting a proportional amount of psychological energy to every object in your domain, whether or not you are aware of it from moment to moment.

Clutter as Tangible Procrastination

In a sense, clutter is the end result of procrastination—especially if your problem is not so much that you have too much stuff, but rather that the stuff you have is disorganized. You know all the anthems of the procrastinator: "I'll start tomorrow," "I need shelves before I can do anything," or even just "I'll do it later."

Clutter arises in a series of moment-by-moment decisions to postpone action. Consider yourself pouring a bowl of cereal. You pour the cereal in the bowl, perhaps spilling a flake or two in the process. Ditto for a drop or two of milk. Something good is on TV, so you head for the couch—leaving behind the open cereal box and milk carton, plus the crumbs and spilled milk. Thus ariseth clutter.

What went on there? At the precise moment that you had a choice about whether to leave a mess, you chose to rush into the next moment. The couch was waiting. You chose the next experience over finishing the one you started. You didn't allow yourself to feel the small satisfaction of closing the lid on the cereal and putting the rest of the stuff away. One more sticky little glob of psychic baggage was added to your unconscious. Coagulate a bunch of these globs together and you will have a messy, cluttered, disorganized home environment.

The alternative to this rush to the next sensation is to savor what's right in front of you. There's a little pulse of satisfaction, contentment, or even beauty in completing what you've started. Learn to fine-tune your antenna that picks up this bit of quiet pleasure, appreciate it, and cultivate it. True, it may be a subtle pleasure—as subtle as the burden each item of clutter added to your life—but if you encourage that pleasure, order will emerge effortlessly.

To the anticipated chorus of excuses that procrastinators offer when action seems imminent, I offer this bit of graffiti that someone etched into wet cement in a Haight-Ashbury sidewalk of San Francisco: "SHUT UP AND DEAL WITH IT." It may not be the most polite bit of advice, but it has a wonderful ring of usefulness about it.

If you would like to get to work and break up your procrastination habits, fortunately there are two excellent and accessible books on the subject, which we have listed in Appendix B, "Resources."

The Slobs vs. the Fussbudgets

The Greeks and the Trojans certainly had their differences. So did the Hatfields and the McCoys. Most of the twentieth century was treated to the Commies and the capitalists. But these struggles pale in comparison to the struggle taking place under the roofs of most households every day. We are talking about the slobs vs. the fussbudgets.

We're not sure if everyone in the world fits into one of these two categories, but it sure seems like most are at least inclined one way or the other. Perhaps you are a slob trying to reform or a fussbudget trying to learn a few new tricks. Either way, you are probably not pleased with the unpleasantness of arguing with the other half of the world.

It can get ugly. There you are, having spent all day Saturday (or considerably less, if you followed *Speed Cleaning*) cleaning the house. It is gleaming. Your significant other arrives home from a triumphant tennis match and drops his or her sweaty clothes on the floor of the closet, within reach of the clothes hamper designed specifically to receive said garments. What are both of these people thinking? Probably something like:

YOU: You don't even realize I just cleaned the house. What a jerk. You did this just to torture me.
SIG. OTHER: Great tennis game. Too bad I had to cheat. I can't wait to get in the shower.

The conversation (if there is one) runs something like this:

YOU: HU-neeeeee! I just cleaned the house, and look at what you're doing!

SIG. OTHER: Huh? Oh, yeah. Looks great. Are there any clean towels?

Not the most satisfying of scenes, is it? So what do you do if you live with a clutterer who is driving you crazy? He or she can tear the kitchen apart to open a can of tuna, will leave the mess behind, and will remain blissfully unaware of any problem. Or what if you live with a fussbudget who is needling you incessantly? He or she wants the dishtowel folded every time it's hung up, or doesn't let the newspaper sit on the floor for ten seconds, or starts to wash the dishes before everyone's finished eating dinner.

First, let's try to lay out the reasoning from each point of view. We are calling each end of this axis by a slightly pejorative term (get over it) to keep it a fair fight: That's exactly how each one views the opposition. The fussbudget perceives acts of sloppiness as deliberate acts—ones carried out spitefully to provoke, to retaliate against, or to torture the fussbudget. The slob perceives acts of tidiness and organization as deliberate attempts to demean, to control, and to reform the slob.

From both points of view, a common theme is that the other's behavior is viewed as highly personal—that is, it appears to be directed specifically at the perceiver. In our saner moments, of course, we know that isn't true. The slob is actually thinking about his or her mean boss, or yesterday's golf game, or tonight's dinner. The fussbudget is really concerned with order or hygiene or cleanliness.

So the first step in dealing with this sort of conflict is to depersonalize it as much as possible. To the extent that you do, you will be able to avoid getting angry. These are events that are happening; in the vast majority of cases, they are not messages beamed directly at your sense of worth as a person. If you are very reflective, you'll notice that there's a split second between when you become aware of something that usually makes you angry and the actual emotional response of anger. In that split second, try to focus on the impersonal nature of the slob's or fussbudget's behavior. Does he or she really have you in mind? Is the person being deliberately malicious? Quite probably not. Keep your attention riveted on that fact, and you'll find that a lot of the emotional steam is taken out of these confrontations. Your friend is probably focusing on his or her own dear self, as is most of the world at any given moment.

Everyone is smack in the middle of his or her own truth. That of the slob, to the slob, is just as valid as the fussbudget's truth. No sense in trying to mess with that. Might as well try asking a tornado to rotate the other way.

What you might have more success with, however, is a dialogue. Leave the words "should" and "ought" behind: They are control-oriented words that ooze rebuke between the lines. Accordingly, they are remarkably unsuccessful as agents of persuasion. You'll have better luck with expression. As the psychologist Albert Ellis is fond of pointing out, "prefer" is a much more workable term. *Tell* the other person how *you* are feeling and what *you* are thinking—not what you are convinced *they* are feeling or thinking. And *ask* the other person what's going on with him or her. Most slobs are sincerely surprised to find that fussbudgets are upset by a half-inch puddle of standing water in the middle of the bathroom. Most fussbudgets think everybody wants ironed underwear.

Humans being the odd creatures we are, if your partner became too similar to you you'd probably squabble even more. Don't try to make the other person into another version of you. It won't work. If you're compassionate and patient, what can emerge is an agreement to move toward each other's way of life at least a little bit, with as much respect and understanding as you can muster. This aiming toward the other person is the important thing, not whether you completely change your ways. If you can pick up the waterlogged towels you've thrown on the bathroom floor, maybe your partner can relax the dishwashing schedule just a bit. And *thank* each other along the way, even if it doesn't come naturally.

What if this idealistic program meets with no success whatsoever? Well, the least you can hope for is to enable the other person to experience directly the consequences of his or her actions. If the slob leaves a trail of clothes all over the house, do you really expect any change if you follow along and pick up after him or her? Things are working out pretty well from the slob's point of view: Why put a perfectly good valet out of commission? But what would happen if the slob's clothes were regularly rounded up and deposited in a bin and left there? Maybe the owner would notice a drastic lack of apparel after a while—at least unrumpled apparel. Until slobs actually feel the consequences of their behavior, there is little chance of success. The same is true for fussbudgets. If your favorite fussbudget is spending all his or her spare time ironing doilies, maybe it would help to point out gently that a picnic is being planned and his or her company would be greatly appreciated.

Action Steps

Here are a few specific suggestions based on behavioral ideas that you might find helpful in dealing with your clutter habit:

• If you are embarrassed to invite others over because the house is in such a mess all the time, as an antidote go ahead and invite people over regularly. Start with once a month, if that helps. It'll be a nudge to get you to clean up your act. Do it often enough, and you'll probably get used to an uncluttered house. So invite someone over for tea or dinner or strip poker. But make sure to rotate guests, because a regular visitor will get used to your mess.

• Your clutter wasn't accumulated in a day, so don't expect it to be resolved in a day. Start with whatever is bothering you the most. Appreciate the progress you make along the way. Setting perfectionist goals will just lead you into cycles of resolution and failed attempts. Accept your less-than-perfect success (and less-than-perfect self!).

• Don't declare "I *am* a collector" any more than you would say "You *are* a bad child." It creates a similar sort of wound. It is not your essence to be a collector. It is what you are *doing* at the moment—not what you are being. If you define yourself as a collector or a junkaholic, it will be that much more difficult to change. You have defined yourself—not described what you are doing, which is a much less loaded question. What you are doing is far more easy to change than your view of yourself.

• Don't toss out a young child's favorite toy (e.g., a teddy bear) without discussing it with the child. A teddy bear is a first love object, and the child could be learning that loved ones can vanish in a rather drastic manner. If a rigid organizational system is imposed in too authoritarian a manner, paradoxically you may end up teaching a child to be a revenge clutterer, according to clutter consultant and instructor Charlene Richter, who is president of Getting Organized, in San Francisco. Their kids becoming slobs was a message to parents to back off and grant them reasonable autonomy—even though the message continued to be sent years and years after the fact.

• Remember that your child is modeling your behavior. The wife of an acquaintance of mine was said never to have thrown away a single issue of any magazine that ever entered the house. One room of the house was devoted almost entirely to huge stacks of magazines that were going to be read "someday." She rinsed out and reused paper towels and aluminum foil. Was it therefore a surprise that her child refused to let go of a single toy, even if it was worn to shreds? When asked to throw away or give away a toy, he would scream "IT'S MINE IT'S MINE IT'S MINE IT'S MINE IT'S MINE" at ear-splitting levels.

• Do you get stuck in the middle of a huge ambivalence when you're trying to decide whether to throw something out? When you're spending a great deal of time teetering back and forth, it seems like this is a very big decision. In truth, if you're spending that much time, it more likely means that there would not be a whole lot of difference in your life if the object stayed or if it didn't. Let it go.

• See how you feel when a room is clutter-free. Sit down in it and percolate awhile. Are you happy as a clam? Or do you feel mildly uncomfortable? If the latter, the clutter will return in short order precisely because you want it to. Stay with this feeling awhile and see if you can see yourself in a clutter-free room and enjoying it. Reflect on the fact that you are entitled to an orderly, beautiful environment no less or no more than anyone else.

• Are there parts of your life that you have successfully organized, especially at the office? Reflect on the skills you already learned in that domain. See if you can shift your opinion of your organizational skills accordingly: You're not a total slob after all! And then apply some of those skills to your home environment.

• Make an appointment with yourself—and then keep it—to spend a fixed and reasonable amount of time decluttering: a serious, write-it-down-in-your-book, don't-miss-it-unless-you're-sick-in-bed kind of appointment. It's the same kind of appointment you would routinely make with a doctor or with an important client at work.

Chapter 3

UNCLUTTERING GUIDES: AN ALPHABETICAL LIST

Sorry, but at this point you're fresh out of excuses: You've learned the rules. You've explored the psychology of clutter. It's time to get down and dirty.

Uncluttering is like putting your home on a diet, and the Uncluttering Guides that follow are the recipes to use to do just that. Like food recipes, they list all the ingredients and procedures you'll need to make the job as clear and painless as possible.

As mentioned before, either start with the area of clutter that's bothering you the most, or at the beginning of the alphabetical list, and work your way through it. Clutter will disappear from the house as it disappears from the list of things that are nagging at you and driving you crazy. The "new" you will emerge—clutter-free, organized, and perhaps just the tiniest bit smug.

ANTICLUTTER EQUIPMENT

Products that will help you unclutter.

CUPBOARDS

1. To help arrange cupboards so that you can see the items stored in the back of the shelves, install tiered shelves you can purchase or make. They are similar to bleachers—different levels arranged so everyone can see over the head of the person in front of them.

2. To make finding a particular spice easier, install shelves the height and depth of one spice container so each spice is visible. Arrange spices alphabetically. The best place to mount this special spice shelf is on the inside door of an eye-level cupboard. If the shelves inside the cupboard make this impossible, the inside of a pantry door may work if you're lucky enough to have a pantry. Otherwise, mount them on a kitchen wall close to the main food-preparation area. Another alternative is a lazy Susan (see number 4).

3. Similar shelves on the inside of other cupboard doors are handy. For example, a metal wire shelf on the inside of the cupboard door under the sink is great for storing the wet sponge and scrub pad plus dishwasher soap and regular dish soap. It makes it so easy to use and retrieve these items that maybe you'll store them here instead of leaving them out as clutter on the counter.

4. A lazy Susan is the next best alternative for storing your spices if you don't have a place to install the shelves mentioned above. Place it at the front of a prime storage shelf. Get the biggest lazy Susan your shelf will accommodate; the one with several different levels is best. Use it just for spices; don't store the salt and pepper shakers or other everyday items here. If you reserve it only for spices, it will at least have a chance to stay organized. Be sure to raise the shelf above the lazy Susan to make enough room to place and remove items behind the lazy Susan without knocking half the spices off.

A lazy Susan is also handy in bathroom cupboards. Use it under the sink to store the overflow from the medicine cabinet—or for all the hundreds of different makeups, powders, ointments, salves, and unguents that one certain household member seems to need. Let that person use this lazy Susan exclusively.

DRAWERS

Rubbermaid makes interlocking plastic boxes in six sizes and shapes that are more versatile than conventional silverware trays for organizing kitchen drawers. They are called "Keepers Drawer Organizers." Use them to divide up the junk in the junk drawer so you can find the screwdriver from among all the rest of the stuff, for a change. Use them to keep the little pieces of your pastry kit from becoming buried at the back of the drawer, or to keep pens and pencils and everything else organized in a desk drawer. Larger types of drawer organizers can be used to divide the socks from the T-shirts in the dresser drawer.

SHOWERS

Get a caddy that loops over the shower head and holds soap, several bottles of shampoo, and a washcloth. It will also provide a spot to hang a squeegee for wiping down the shower walls once a day, which will help prevent soap and hard-water buildup.

CLOSETS

1. Add a second pole under the existing one for a second layer of shirt- or jacket-length clothes. It requires little more than measuring and drawing where you want it to be, going to the hardware store for the pole and brackets, and finding a drill and a screwdriver to install it.

BEFORE   AFTER!

2. Instead of a second pole, or in addition to it, put stackable vented plastic storage boxes or open basket drawers under your existing pole for extra storage of folded clothing, socks, and shoes.

3. Put up as many hooks as you have room for. They're great for hanging clothes that aren't quite ready for the laundry, for pajamas, your favorite belt, scarves, purses, or bathrobe. You can purchase groups of six or more plastic hooks that can all be installed with just two screws. Don't forget to do the same thing in the kids' closets.

4. Add a shelf if there is wasted storage space above the existing shelf in your closet. One more high shelf is great for Christmas decorations, winter clothes in the summer, and summer clothes in the winter. Adding shelves in a tall, skinny utility closet can add much more storage space. Install shelves above the height of the broom and mop you have stored there. Alternatively, install shelves from top to bottom, and store the broom and mop on hooks on the inside of the closet door. This turns it into a pantry if you need a pantry worse than a utility closet. (See the section "Garage Shelves," page 91.)

GENERAL STORAGE

1. Tool or tackle boxes are good for the kids' art supplies, your own sewing supplies, or other small items. The newer plastic ones can cost less than $10 and, when not used for fishing tackle or heavy tools, will last indefinitely.

2. A small basket on the kitchen counter is good for tossing the coupons you want to save. A tall basket in the closet for the dry cleaning helps with something that's hard to get together at the last minute. Careful, though: Baskets seem addictive to some people, and they can quickly change from useful storage to clutter.

3. A small chest will often fit under the jacket-length clothes in the closet and can be used to store just about anything.

BIRTHDAYS

No more belated cards!

Have trouble remembering friends' and relatives' birthdays? Do you leave yourself little reminder notes and then discover them too late? Wouldn't it be nice to have enough time to pick up a card or gift without making a special trip? The solution is relatively painless—at least far less painful than the repercussions of forgetting certain people's birthdays!

On New Year's Day, sit down with your address book or computerized address file. Take out your new calendar for that year. Take a fat red pen or pencil in hand and write the name of every person you want to remember in the appropriate box (or line) in the calendar. If the person is out of state, you might want to record a warning for yourself a week or so ahead: "Mail Uncle Rufus's BD card." The same precaution applies if the person's birthday is early in the month and will be lurking out of sight on the next page of the calendar.

Apply this simple technique, and your friends and relations will marvel at your memory. You'll know better, but don't let on.

CHILDREN'S ROOMS

Organizing the room so the children will be.

Two schools of thought apply. The first one is by far the simpler. Control the clutter in the kids' rooms by closing the door and keeping it closed. Never go in the room. Never even look in the room. Deposit clean clothes and other necessities outside the door the same way food is deposited outside a jail cell. If you avoid even fleeting glimpses of these rooms, you may be able to enjoy at least the illusion that your home is organized and clutter-free. If you can't (or won't), let's get to work on the second school of thought.

GIVING THEM A CHANCE TO SUCCEED

One genuine excuse kids have for not hanging up their clothes is that they can't reach the rods in the closets. Lower the rods to a height that allows them to be reached. Ditto for hooks to hang things on. Both of these items are usually easy to raise or lower. If the rod is difficult or inconvenient to move, leave it in place and install a new rod at a lower level. Both the brackets and the rod are quite inexpensive and are available at hardware stores. Raise them over the years as the kids grow. In the meantime, use those higher areas for storage.

Get a nice big basket for their dirty clothes and an oversized waste-basket for trash. The bigger and the lower these baskets are, the better your odds are that they'll actually be used. You can also use plastic baskets for toys and games. Baskets can also be used for clean clothes if you don't have enough drawer space or if the kids can't reach the drawers. Inexpensive plastic tool or tackle boxes are great for things such as crayons, art supplies, and other collections of smaller toys or supplies.

Once you have installed the necessary boxes and baskets and have lowered the rods and hangers in the closet, label all these items according to their purpose. Use words or pictures, depending upon the age of the child. Also label shelves, drawers, and cupboards.

If you're short on space in the kids' rooms, you might consider an investment in a captain's bed (a platform bed with built-in drawers under the mattress). Or add-on drawers can be installed under conventional mattress frames.

IS IT WORTH THE STRUGGLE?

This sounds like a lot of work for you. Is it really worth the effort? Even after you do the organizing, the really hard part will be to teach the kids actually to use all these organizational tools. Our two cents' worth is yes, it's worth it. Children want to learn. Doing everything for them is far from beneficial. The competence you hope they'll have later in life as adults starts with learning and acquiring skills sooner or later. Sooner seems better.

CLOSETS, BASEMENTS, GARAGES, AND ATTICS

How to clean them out step by step.

This guide focuses on closets, but it works just as well on a larger scale for cleaning out the basement, garage, or attic. It's one of your best allies in the eventual victory over clutter.

Go ahead and feel sorry for yourself if you want to. Apparently few people like to do this except when they're depressed. Remember Mary Tyler Moore (as Mary Richards), who was forever cleaning closets and drawers when she felt blue? You're not alone in your dread of the giant can of worms this job may open. However, the payoff is great and the sense of accomplishment splendid, so please persevere.

SUPPLIES

Four to seven medium or large cardboard boxes. The exact number will depend upon the amount of stuff—especially whatever will be leaving your house when you're finished with this job. (You may substitute large plastic garbage bags instead—especially if not having any boxes will be used as an excuse—but they're harder to toss things into.)

It's best to do this while home alone—in part because you're going to need a large area to work in, but mainly because some difficult decisions will have to be made. Don't invite any more angst by assembling a committee to vote on all the stuff you're going to review. The benevolent dictator approach is much preferred. (Veto rights for those affected are optional.) Start this job early in the day because it's time-consuming and you're undoubtedly going to be interrupted.

Getting started is probably the most difficult part of this job. You have an inkling of what faces you and what a big mess you'll find when you start exploring corners of the closet that haven't seen the light of day for years. Be brave. First just place the cardboard boxes outside the closet in a semicircle, if possible. You're going to use these boxes to sort the items you remove from the closet. Label the boxes with a marking pen as follows:

1. Trash
2. Garage Sale or Charity
3. Belongs Elsewhere
4. Not Sure

5. Return to Owner
6. Repair
7. Altering or Mending

Notice that none of your choices includes a box labeled "Move to the Attic or Garage." Box 3 is for an item you find in the closet that belongs in the kitchen, for example. Don't use box 3 as a sleazy excuse to shuffle items elsewhere in your house.

The plan is to empty the closet completely. Remove most items one at a time, not in big armfuls, and as you remove each item, plop it in the appropriate box. Remove even the things that rightfully belong here. You'll replace them a bit later. (Resist the impulse to paint the closet after it's empty: You'll decide you've done enough and put all the stuff right back in.)

So, for example, as you take out clothes, you may come across the sweater that you looked great in—before one spaghetti meal stained it and cumulative spaghetti meals had their impact on you. With a light heart, put it into the box marked "Trash" or "Charity." (See Rule 2: "Use it or lose it.")

When you come to the overnight bag in search of which your son tore the house apart twice, drop it in box 3—("Belongs Elsewhere"). Later you can store it with the rest of the luggage. (See Rule 3: "Efficiency counts, so store things accordingly.")

When you come to the unused, never-even-taken-out-of-the-box attachments to the vacuum that you traded in three years ago, put it in box 1 ("Trash"). Let's be very clear at this point: There is *no doubt* about tossing attachments for which you no longer have a vacuum. This is an *easy* decision. Right?

When you ultimately find six purses that exceed the number of purses you picked according to Rule 6 ("Pick a number and stick with it"), you'll have to decide which ones to keep and which ones to toss. But don't do that now. Just put them in box 4 and continue grabbing items one at a time from the closet.

When you come across your college psychology textbook (circa 1958) that you still believe, albeit by habit, you will refer to someday, you can easily be thrown into a panic. How can you possibly decide what to do with such books right this second? After all, you've been saving them for years, and you can't undo that decision without lengthy deliberation. No problem. Just plop them into box 4 ("Not Sure") and proceed.

Items you've been saving because they need repair generally belong in box 1. Keep them only if you make a special box for them (box 6) and promise actually to take them to be repaired.

The same goes for clothes that need to be mended or altered. You can't continue to save them and use the excuse that you're waiting until you know someone who will do this work for you. No one knows this person. Instead, look in the yellow pages under "Tailors" or "Dressmakers" (not "Alterations" or "Mending"). Take a chance with one of the listings and make an appointment. Put those items in box 7. When that box is full and you realize how much it's going to cost to mend clothes you haven't even missed, cancel your appointment and change the box label to "Charity."

In sorting through the closet, we are proposing that you make decisions for the rest of the family. When you run into someone else's stuff, don't put it in box 4 ("Not Sure") every time, or you'll defeat the whole process. The rest of the household may not have your same concern about reducing clutter or reclaiming storage area. Apply the rules for controlling clutter to their possessions exactly as you would to yours. One teensy little warning: Years from now, you may be accused by your children of causing them permanent psychological damage when you threw away their Lionel train set, Mickey Mouse Club membership card, or picture of Paul McCartney. If you would like to be extremely fair, announce one or two weeks prior to your starting this job that you intend to get rid of all unused stuff, no matter who it belongs to. Promulgate this warning along with serene assurances that they may retrieve any wanted items before you start the job. Otherwise they forswear the right to complain after you've thrown out or given away something of theirs. As you well know, it's very unlikely that anyone is going to go excavating through the closet in the armistice period. But at least you'll have a free hand and peace of mind as you sort through and make decisions about their possessions.

It's clear that the hardest part of this job is discarding things. We won't be flip about how difficult it is to make decisions to part with items that have fond memories associated with them or that otherwise seem truly valuable to you. Here are some guidelines to help your decision-making:

1. Some sentimental things can and should be saved. You're only human. However, there are limits. You're not going to forget your own wedding even if you give away your wedding dress. And some sentimental items can be saved in a different form. For example, take a picture of yourself holding your college tennis racket for one last time (it hasn't touched a tennis ball in twenty-two years), and then let the racket go to someone who will use it.

2. If you don't make some hard decisions and get rid of many items, you'll have as much stuff when you finish cleaning the closet as when you started. It may end up in different parts of the house, but your overall clutter inventory will only be redistributed, not reduced. Not exactly a wildly successful job of closet cleaning.

3. When you find yourself coming to item after item that you don't want to part with for which you're willing to break a rule, remember why you started this project in the first place. The clutter has bothered you, is bothering you, and will continue to bother you. Believe us (and the man in the "Dear Abby" letter in Chapter 1) that you will not miss these items when they're gone. For ages you hadn't thought of many of the items you're rediscovering. Had you not been cleaning out the closet, you wouldn't be thinking about them now. And you're not going to think of them again tomorrow. Honest.

Put the items to go back into the closet on the floor next to the boxes. Once the closet is empty, but before you move the boxes or start to reload the closet, first turn your attention to box 4 ("Not Sure"). Don't put this box off until last. If you do, you may run out of patience for the hard decisions required for it. The temptation will be just to slide the box right back into the closet. Besides, you still have boxes 1 and 2 close at hand. Hopefully you'll feel so good from successfully parting with some stuff that you'll transfer most of the items from Not Sure box into the boxes leaving the house and starting a new life elsewhere.

The next step is to take the remaining boxes to their appropriate places. If the recipients of the Charity box or boxes will pick them up, call and schedule it. Otherwise, load them into your car *now* and deliver them. *Don't put the boxes in the garage.* That's too dangerous. Far too often, the boxes become permanent fixtures in that new location. Sooner or later someone will have to go through all this sorting again because no one will remember what's in the boxes, or someone will go through each box to see if he or she agrees with your decisions.

Take box 3 ("Belongs Elsewhere") and distribute those items where they belong. This step can have the somewhat disconcerting effect of causing an overflow elsewhere. No matter. You can tackle that area when you're ready.

Finally, put what's left back into the closet. The reason you save this step for last is because it is by far the easiest. But there are rules about how to replace these items. When replacing clothes, there are several levels of organization that will save you time dressing each morning. First, separate items for above the waist from those for below the waist. Within those categories, put like items together, such as skirts, pants, jackets, shirts, and accessories. Hang suits with suits and dresses with dresses. Put hangers all in the same direction. Toss your extra supply of hangers, or recycle them with a local thrift shop.

Many closets in newer homes already have an additional pole for hanging clothes at a second level. It's an easy project to add one, and there's room in almost all closets to add a pole under the shirt or blouse section. Go to a lumber yard or a full-service hardware store after measuring the required length. Make a sketch for the salesperson, and he or she should be able to send you back home with everything you'll need. (See the section "Anticlutter Equipment," page 57.) Add-on poles are also sold ready-made.

Some closets are apt to look practically empty once you get them organized. The feeling of being able to find what you're looking for—let alone the luxury of a little extra space for a change—more than compensates for having your "nest" a bit less full.

COLLECTIBLES

It's okay to "uncollect" a collection.

A COLLECTION IS BORN

It's startling how some inanimate objects seem to reproduce as if they were the real thing instead of replicas. Over time, rather than a frog sitting peacefully (and alone) on your bookshelf, there are so many frogs of various sizes and shapes that you've got a "collection"—even though you may never have intended to create one—and you are a "collector"—even though you don't feel any different. All you did was buy one little porcelain frog at a curio shop while on vacation a few years ago.

IT GROWS AND GROWS AND GROWS

Later a friend or relative noticed the frog sitting on your bookshelf and decided on your Christmas gift then and there. You accepted the gift of a second frog (what else are you going to do?) and put the new frog next to the original. Now that there were two of them sitting side by side, it was twice as likely that other people would get you more frog gifts. As the number of frogs grew, the likelihood of getting more increased exponentially, and before long you have more frogs than a June pond—most of which aren't nearly as nice as the one really wonderful original that you selected yourself.

Once in place, this collection can't be ignored. For starters, after there are a certain number of them they may be the most striking feature of an entire room. Unfortunately, it will usually be in a way that has nothing whatever to do with your original design scheme. They also require dusting and cleaning— neither of which is all that quick, because each one must be picked up and replaced to do so. They have truly become clutter in one of its more straightforward forms.

Have a garage sale, or give the entire collection to a charity or nursing or convalescent home. Or you could do what game wardens call "harvesting." They harvest to reduce the size of a herd of animals when there are too many of a species in one area to be supported by the amount of food available. In this case, reduce the size of your collection by half or two thirds. Afterward tell everyone that you wanted to share their beauty with others who would enjoy them. And also don't forget to tell them that you are no longer "collecting" frogs!

IF YOU LOVE YOUR COLLECTION

Naturally, the above strategy doesn't apply if your collection is your pride and joy. It may still be clutter in the eyes of others, but as long as you enjoy it, don't worry what others may think. You can make it easier to maintain your collection (and to keep it contained) by putting it in a display case so it doesn't get dusty and dirty.

CUPBOARDS AND DRAWERS

How to organize cupboards and drawers.

ORGANIZED ≠ NEAT

Being neat is entirely different from being organized. An alphabetized kitchen with everything in order is neat as a pin but totally disorganized. It's how you use something and not its relative position in the alphabet that matters when organizing. There are few absolutes. We're going to offer you some conventional wisdom and guidelines on the subject of organizing cupboards and drawers. You may decide to ignore our advice. That's fine. Follow your instincts and use a unique system of your own. If your system works correctly, you'll be getting the most storage possible from your available space. In addition, you'll be able to locate things easily and can tell at a glance what you're about to run out of. However, no system will work if no one else knows about it or if you can't find things when you need them.

CUPBOARDS

We're going to talk about cupboards first, then drawers. Much of what applies to cupboards also applies to drawers, so read both sections even if you're only interested in organizing the latter. Also, since there are more cupboards and drawers in the kitchen than in any other room, we'll use the kitchen for most of our examples. But use these ideas for organizing cupboards and drawers no matter where they're located in your home. Products to help you expand your storage space or to help keep things organized are discussed under "Anticlutter Equipment" on page 57.

Like Items Together?

In general, most organizers advise you to organize within drawers and cupboards by like item. That's not entirely helpful in and of itself. I mean, how many like items do you have? Take a bag of sugar, for example. Nothing else in your kitchen is exactly "like" a bag of sugar. So the first step in organizing is to strrrrrrretch the normally accepted definition of "like items." You may decide that a bag of flour is like a bag of sugar because they are both a basic foodstuff. It would be just as correct if I decide to store the sugar with the coffee. They seem more alike to me because I think of them together. Some people might store the cold cereal next to the sugar: After all, they're both dry and can be packaged in a similarly shaped box. You get the idea. *Make associations that make sense to you.*

Here are some conventional ideas for grouping similar items. Store basics such as flour and sugar together, canned goods together, then soups and other subdivisions together within that group. Rice, dry beans, macaroni, and spaghetti may belong together. Put packaged preparations such as salad-dressing mix and taco mix together. In cupboards full of dishes, it's usually easy to store like items together. Even then, don't forget to stretch the meaning of like items if it suits you. For example, you don't have to store the water glasses in the same cupboard with the coffee mugs if the coffee maker is on the other side of the room. Locate the coffee mugs in a cupboard close to the coffee maker instead.

You may decide to store items together that aren't alike but are used together. If you've taken up Chinese cooking, store all that gear together. If you have several favorite meals, you can store the items used to make each meal together (e.g., tomato paste, tomato sauce, oregano, and pasta). Or group together all the tools and supplies you use when you barbecue. Or put all the waxes, cleaners, cloths, and sponges used to wash the car together in the dishpan or bucket you use to hold the cleaning solution.

Once you've decided on the like items that go together, then what? Do you leave the rest of the cupboard empty once you run out of like items? Obviously not, but you need to stretch the definition of like items even farther to decide which items go next to a completed group of similar items (e.g., what goes next to the flour and the sugar). Here's another place where your first impulse can guide you. Pick things to go together within a cupboard or drawer that seem logical to you. And consider frequency of use and size of the items as you make your decisions. Let's talk about frequency first.

Prime Storage

There is a pecking order among the shelves in a cupboard. As we said in discussing Rule 3, "hot" items go in "hot" spots. Prime storage space is the most visible and easiest place to store or retrieve something. It is most definitely not a prime storage spot if getting a certain item in or out of it can throw your back out for a week. For example, my mother stores her vacuum in a spot that's so inaccessible that she practically has to move the television to get it out. The shelves at eye level are prime storage space, and the ones progressively higher or lower are less and less desirable. The same goes for drawers. Top drawers are prime, and the lowest drawer is the least appealing as a storage place. In the kitchen and bathroom, you can even use the countertop itself as prime storage space.

Your job is to match the things you use most often with prime storage areas. For example, ready-to-use foods such as cereal should have a prime location. So should the things you use every day, such as plates, glasses, pots, and pans. The dedicated soufflé casserole or the special pot you use once a year for your not-yet-world-famous chili should not. But also take a hard look at some of the appliances you leave out. When was the last time you used the fourteen-speed turboblender? If it was months ago, put it and any other similarly neglected appliances away in "cooler" storage.

Organize only by function, and try not to consider form. Don't leave on the countertop a set of canisters full of things you seldom use, even if they look nice there. They just add to the clutter. If you don't use the things in them very often, put them in a lower or a higher cupboard. But if you really love your canister set and don't want to store it out of sight, use the canisters to store granola, cookies, and other family favorites—and ignore the labels "flour," "sugar," "coffee," and "tea" printed on their sides. (Or turn the labels to the wall.)

SIZE COUNTS, TOO

The height or bulk of an item is the final factor to consider. You do so for the same reason you position shorter people in the front row of a group photo—so you can see all the people in the picture. The payoff is that you don't have to move half the items stored on a particular shelf in an attempt to find what you're looking for. If you store tall and bulky items in the back and progressively shorter things toward the front, you can see at a glance what you're looking for. This is more difficult than it sounds, because the items you're organizing may not differ enough in height. There are also some ideas for solving this problem under "Anticlutter Equipment."

You can vary this directive if you own many tall items and just a few short ones. Store tall things in the back and on one or both sides of the cupboard, and reserve only the middle area for short things.

Spices

Ever notice how easy it is to find a particular spice at the grocery store? They are arranged alphabetically on a shelf that allows you to see each spice container easily. Arrange yours in a similar way or on a lazy Susan. For more help on this subject, see the section "Anticlutter Equipment."

DRAWERS

Drawers tend to disintegrate into chaos quickly. One reason for this unhappy event is that drawers have a kind of automatic self-packing design. Every time someone slams a drawer shut, everything in that drawer goes flying to the back of the drawer. Unless that stuff is rearranged to the front regularly, after a while it becomes unused and forgotten. In effect, what's in the back is really only useful for keeping the things in the front from sliding farther back. In addition, you can pack more things into drawers than is wise because what's in it won't fall out when you open it (assuming you *can* still open it), as it would if you loaded a cupboard the same way. All the more reason to try to get the drawers organized.

Follow the same strategies we discussed for cupboards. Start by trying to organize like items together. Put the most frequently used items in the prime top drawers. Many of the things you store in drawers are utensils with handles, and it's hard to recognize each utensil by the handle alone. You can make it easier to spot what you're looking for by storing the handles toward the back of the drawer. Now it's easy to see the difference between a spatula or a serving spoon that have a similar handle.

Drawers—and not just the silverware drawer—need dividers. This applies to drawers full of cooking utensils, linen, and even junk. Dividers keep things organized, save you time locating items, and keep things from compressing to the back of the drawer. For more information, once again we refer you to "Anticlutter Equipment," page 57.

DUPLICATES

Some things you actually need more of!

It's hard to admit, in a book about controlling clutter, that we want you to haul more things into the house. Duplicates of certain things, however, can save you time and make your life less cluttered and more in control.

Humorist, raconteur, and wit Art Buchwald is quoted as saying, "The one item you need to complete a chore is downstairs when you are upstairs, and upstairs when you are downstairs."[1] Whether you have stairs or not, if this type of problem arises regularly, you should consider duplicating certain items to solve it and to make your life a bit simpler.

Vacuuming is usually not that difficult a job. Getting the vacuum itself out of storage or hauling it up and down stairs can be the annoying and tiring part of the job. We already recommended that you store the vacuum in a convenient place (Rule 3, "Efficiency counts, so store things accordingly"). But if you have an upstairs and a downstairs to vacuum, consider acquiring an upstairs and a downstairs vacuum. If other areas pose a problem—such as near the door from the garden—a hand-held portable vacuum may be just the thing. (Keep it near the problem area, not away in a closet.)

If you're like many people, when you're in the bathroom and getting ready to go somewhere, you're quite interested in what time it is so you won't be late. And it's one of the least likely rooms to have a clock! So add one. A travel clock that you'll use occasionally on trips only costs about $10. Or stick one of those very inexpensive digital clocks on the mirror. It reduces stress, and it saves you from having to leave the room to go somewhere else to check the time.

1. *The Saturday Evening Post* (July/August 1986), p. 28.

Several small items are easily and inexpensively duplicated. Put scissors in the kitchen, in your desk, and in your bathroom. Put fingernail clippers in your purse and the bathroom drawer. Put a folding umbrella under the driver's seat in the car. It will avoid all those infuriating times when it starts raining and you don't have an umbrella with you—despite the fact that you own half a dozen of them.

A loose (unmarked) house key in your pocket guarantees that you won't have a real emergency on your hands if you lose your entire ring of keys. At least you can get into the house again. Do something similar with the door (not ignition) key to your car: Put it in a magnetized key box that attaches to your car in a concealed spot. In case the keys get locked inside your car, it's comforting to know you won't have to call a locksmith or break a window to get in.

This is far from a comprehensive list. You'll think of other things that always seem to be in the wrong place. That's the acid test. If you need something that always seems to be in the wrong place, consider duplicating it—especially if it's inexpensive.

FILE CABINETS

How to set up a household file cabinet.

Many desks have one or more drawers designed to accept hanging files. If you're considering purchasing both a desk *and* a file cabinet, select the desk first: You may find one that has a built-in file cabinet. Also, please see Rule 7, on page 27, for more information on selecting a file cabinet.

If you have a desk, position your new file cabinet next to it. The cabinet should be situated so you can open and close the drawers without moving your desk chair.

An indispensable component of a filing system is a set of hanging folders. Hanging folders ride on two metal "ears"—one on either side of the folder. Each ear hooks over a thin metal side rail, which enables the hanging folder to slide easily. Some newer file cabinets have these rails built in. If not, it's easy to add a metal frame to an existing file-cabinet drawer.

INSTALLING THE METAL FRAMES

Add-on frames have two sets of components. First are the two end braces that fit at the front and back of each drawer. There are also two long, thin, metal side rails that run from the front to the back of the drawer—one on each side. These rails fit in the slots underneath the screw or wing nut of the end braces in front and back. (The assembly procedure is entirely uncomplicated, despite what it sounds like when it's written.) The one little grief here is that these side rails are often too long for the drawer and must be shortened. They are designed to be broken to match the correct length.

To measure for the correct length, loosely install the end braces and side rails in one drawer. Make sure the end braces are all the way to the front and back of the drawer. (The one in the back should be behind the adjustable bookend-type of plate known as a "file follower.") Mark the correct length on just one of the side rails, because all the others will be the same length. Disassemble the frame to do the shortening. You'll notice that one end is notched every ¼ inch or so. The idea is to bend the metal back and forth until it breaks at the appropriate notch. Use two pairs of pliers to bend the metal. Firmly grasp the metal with one pair of pliers on each side of the notch closest to the proper length, and bend the shorter end back and forth until the metal breaks. This can require a fair amount of effort, but the metal is soft enough to break eventually. It is simpler to use a hacksaw if you have one handy, or just bend the extra length at a right angle to get it out of the way.

SETTING UP A FILING SYSTEM

In general, file according to use, not strictly in alphabetical order. For example, put the files you use most often in the front of the top drawer. Examples are files that you work with on an ongoing basis—the "Bills" file you use regularly to pay, and the "Checking" file you remove when you balance your checkbook against your bank statement. Continue toward the back of the drawer with files you use less and less often—such as old tax returns or insurance policies you seldom review. Put bulky, seldom-used files in the very back of the drawer where they are harder to get to or remove—especially if you have a file cabinet whose drawers don't fully extend. For example, I put all the photos that haven't made it into an album yet in this back file. I can open the drawer far enough to stuff more photos into it, and that big, bulky file helps keep the other files in front, where they belong.

Once you have a number of files, it can become difficult to continue filing according to use. In this case, a combination of both usage and the alphabet can be helpful—that is, alphabetize when you get to the seldom-used files, and keep the "hot" files near the front in order of usefulness.

Now it's time to start deciding how to divide up all the items you have into separate files. We've listed some ideas below, but you don't have to make any final decisions yet. First gather all the things you want in the cabinet. Put that stuff into separate stacks you plan on storing as separate files. Hanging files come in two thicknesses: standard (which holds up to ¾ inch or so of papers) or wide-bottom (which holds up to 2 inches or so of papers). If you try to overstuff the standard files, the contents will start to stick out of the top and get frayed when the drawer opens and closes. Overstuffed files also make it difficult to see the identifying tags for the other files.

As you sort, if one stack gets bigger than 2 inches, find a way to divide it again, and turn it into two or more smaller stacks. For example, if all your bills thrown into a single file will be too jammed, establish a separate file, "Credit Card Bills," and put the rest of the bills in a second file, "Bills." Print a very short description on the paper label and insert it into the plastic tab that comes with the hanging files. The plastic tab has two wings that attach to the hanging file by inserting them one wing at a time into a slot at the top of the hanging file. Stagger these labels by inserting the tabs into different slots so you can see them all when you open the drawer. Keep a few extra files, with blank tabs already inserted, at the back of the file cabinet. That will make it much more likely you'll actually start a new file, when needed, rather than add to a pile of clutter elsewhere.

SOME IDEAS FOR FILE NAMES

• Archives: Wills, insurance policies, other important papers (many of which will be duplicates of the originals in a safe-deposit box, if you have one).

- Articles: These are articles you haven't read yet. For articles you want to keep after reading, file them in their own file by subject (e.g., "Garden").
- Automobile
- Bills
- Catalogs
- Checking Account(s)
- Correspondence
- Coupons
- Diskettes
- Humor: This is one you'll enjoy revisiting.
- Individuals (by name): One file for each household member.
- Instruction Manuals
- Personal
- Photographs: Photos before they get installed in an album.
- Product Information
- Savings Account(s)
- School Papers
- Stamps
- Stationery
- Taxes: See the section "Recordkeeping," page 131.
- Things to Do
- Things to File: If you find yourself being indecisive about where to file something, pop it in here; just don't let it get out of hand—review its contents regularly.

- Tickler: Paperwork for items listed on the calendar (e.g., paperwork for the car's registration), invitations for the month so you'll have the address and time handy, and appointments for the month; it's a good place to file reminders and lists.

If you have room, unorthodox things such as spare batteries, rolls of tape, and pens and pencils all fit nicely into files. It makes it easy to remember where such items are because you can file them by name. You can even file books such as a dictionary or photo albums that you want to keep close at hand. Be imaginative and you'll get the most out of this file. Notice, however, that there is no "Miscellaneous" file. That can work too much like a junk drawer. If you decide to have one, keep it small and weed it regularly.

As with organizing cupboards, drawers, closets, etc., we encourage you to follow your first impulses for creating files: They are apt to serve you better than our ideas if ours don't seem to "fit." The test of the system is to be able to retrieve something again—not where or under what name you have it filed. So give files names that have an immediate association for you.

Most office workers put the papers for each file into one or more manila folders and then put the manila folders into the hanging file. There are several good reasons for doing this. It's easier to take just one manila folder in and out of your file than the hanging file itself. In addition, you'll always know where to replace the manila folder because the hanging file with its identifying tag is still in place. Moreover, the manila folders enable you to split a hanging file into convenient subcategories. For example, in the "Automobile" file you might have separate manila folders for "Receipts," "Estimates," "Instructions," and "Documents." Or you can separate the "Bills" file into its individual components ("Telephone," "Utilities," "Garbage," "Water," etc.). You'll know when the hanging file gets too complex to handle without manila folders: You'll be rummaging too much.

IF YOU HAVE NO DESK

If you're using the dining room table as your desk and the file cabinet isn't close to that table, put an expandable file folder in the front of your cabinet. In it put all the files you use regularly: "Bills," "Appointments," "Checking Account," etc. When it's time to pay bills or balance your checking account, remove the entire expandable folder and take it to the dining room table. You now have all the necessary files with you to complete the task at hand without making exasperating trips back to the file cabinet.

A CALCULATOR

As long as you've gone this far, get a calculator—a real one that disgorges a paper output. It saves time and aggravation and is indispensable when you're balancing your checkbook. If you're like most of us, you don't much care for that chore—especially since it never seems to balance on the first or second try. It's amazing how much faster you'll be able to find *your* error (sorry) when you can see the calculations on paper. It's very difficult to find mistakes in, or even trust, totals you can't double-check visually.

GARAGE SHELVES

How to put shelves in the garage even if you don't know a hammer from a screwdriver.

There are plenty of companies these days that will install an entire system of shelves, cupboards, closets, and benches in your garage. (Look under "Shelving" in the yellow pages.) These companies are great, and we encourage you to make use of them if you want to spend the money. If you don't, here's an inexpensive, effective design. It will provide additional storage space to solve the clutter problem in your garage and make some room for the things you want out of the house. This guide is not just for men. It's easy enough that, even without carpentry experience, a person of either gender will have a reasonable time of it.

The total cost will depend on the number of shelves, of course, but $20 to $100 should provide anywhere from a few shelves to a double garage full of them.

SUPPLIES

1. Pressed-board shelves 15 to 18 inches wide.
2. Shelf brackets.
3. Screws.
4. Cordless screwdriver or drill motor.
5. Tape measure.
6. A friendly, preferably tall assistant.
7. A 3- or 4-foot carpenter's level (optional).
8. Three additional shelf brackets for long items (optional).
9. A 1- by 4-inch board and hooks for long-handled tools (optional).

The shelves you are going to install are relatively narrow—15 to 18 inches deep. The 2- or 3-foot deep shelves that many people install in garages are entirely too deep for efficient storage. With shelves that deep, often you can't reach or even see what's in back. So the back of the shelves fill up with things that are never used and become forgotten. This breaks too many rules for our comfort. Besides, 15- to 18-inch shelves are narrow enough to put on more than one wall of the garage and still have plenty of room to get in and out of the car.

SHELVES

Once you've decided which walls to put the shelves on, figure out how many shelves to put on each wall. Install the shelves 12 to 18 inches apart unless you have specific storage requirements for more space. If appropriate, leave a larger space between the floor and the first shelf for larger items, such as garbage cans. If you don't need this extra room, locate the first shelf about 2 feet above the floor. Use the space between the top shelf and the ceiling for large, bulky items such as sleeping bags or light luggage. Look at some of the things you're going to be storing on the shelves and measure them. This will help you decide how far apart to put them.

In general, the gap between the lower two shelves should be about 18 inches, to accommodate heavier items. The higher shelves are typically spaced at 12 inches for smaller and lighter items. (See illustration, page 94.)

Shelves that run all the way from one corner to the other are the most stable because the corners prevent the shelves from jiggling sideways and because they have an extra bracket that provides additional strength.

Measure the length of each shelf you're going to install, and keep a list. These measurements must be accurate, so you or your assistant should double-check them. At this point it wouldn't hurt to make a primitive sketch of your overall design. The sketch will be quite handy when you're trying to explain yourself to the patient people at the lumber yard or hardware store. And it will probably save you a trip or two across town.

BRACKETS

You'll mount the shelves on brackets that screw into the wall's studs. Studs are the vertical members that form the main support component of a wall, usually 2- by 4-inch or 2- by 6-inch wood or steel members. If the walls of your garage aren't finished, you'll be able to see the studs. If the walls have been finished, the most common material is gypsum board (also known as drywall or plasterboard or Sheetrock).

The construction of most garage walls is rough enough to be able to determine the location of the studs by sight. Just find where the vertical rows of nails or screws are that attach the gypsum board to the studs. If you can't see these rows of nails or screws, there are gadgets that can locate them for you. An example is the Studsensor, manufactured by Zircon. It's about the size of a TV remote control, and when you move it slowly over a wall, it lights up as it passes over a wall stud.

Each shelf will be supported by a bracket screwed into every other stud, so count the number of brackets you'll need for each shelf and add that number to your shopping list. Don't forget an extra bracket for each shelf that begins or ends in a corner.

If you're storing particularly heavy items (e.g., entire shelves of full paint cans, car batteries, or electric motors), install brackets on every stud instead of every other. Now it's time to go to the store.

You may have to visit two different stores. First go to a lumber yard for the pressed-board shelves. There's a beveled edge on the front of each shelf, and they come in varying lengths and widths. Pressed-board shelves are available in different grades. The best grade is the smoothest. If you're planning on painting the shelves, get the smoothest type.

Besides the grade of the shelf, discuss your shelf measurements with whomever waits on you. Find out in what lengths the pressed board is available. It's simplest if you can buy a single piece of pressed board cut to the desired measurement for each shelf. However, if your shelves are longer than the longest length of pressed board available, you'll need two pieces of pressed board per shelf. If so, add two extra brackets to your list for each such shelf, as they'll need extra support. Finally, now that you know the price of the pressed board, you can decide on the width of the shelves (usually 15 to 18 inches) if you haven't already done so.

There's no saw listed in the "Supplies" list because you're going to pay the lumber yard to cut your shelves (typically $0.50 to $1.00 per cut). It's well worth the extra cost: The cuts are a true 90 degrees, and they can do it in about one fiftieth the time it would take you.

If the lumber yard doesn't sell the brackets you need, then head over to the hardware store. Along with the total number of brackets on your list, tell the salesperson how wide the pressed board is and how you'll be mounting the brackets (i.e., directly into wood studs, or through gypsum board to wood studs). Now the salesperson will know what size brackets you need and the size and length of screws as well. We think self-tapping steel drywall screws are easiest to use. The screw should sink into the stud at least 1 inch to assure adequate stability. The screws that anchor the bracket to the shelf itself will be shorter than screws that go into the stud. Half-inch screws will probably be what the salesperson recommends for the shelf screws.

A cordless screwdriver or variable-speed, reversible drill motor is essential for this project unless you have the forearms of a gorilla. If you don't have either tool, borrow, rent, or purchase one. The same goes for an assistant.

INSTALLATION

Back at home, start by marking where the lower shelf will go, and work your way up. Measure from the ceiling down to where you want the bottom shelf, and put a pencil mark at that point. Take that same measurement every few feet for the length of the shelf, and make a mark at each measurement. Then take a straight edge (a yardstick, a level, or even one of the shelves) and connect all the marks together into a solid line that shows where the first shelf goes. If you own a carpenter's level, use it after your first measurement from the ceiling to make the line for the shelf. With or without a level, however, as long as you measure accurately, your shelves will be as level as your ceiling. Don't worry about the line you're drawing on the wall: It won't be visible once the shelf is installed.

Then measure from the ceiling down to where you want the second lowest shelf, and make a line there. Continue for as many shelves as you'll be installing—always measuring from the ceiling to avoid cumulative errors in measurement.

When you've drawn a line for each shelf, you're ready to install the first shelf bracket. Start at the top and work down, so when you work on the second shelf the first one won't be in your way. Locate the first wall stud at one end of the shelf. Hold a bracket over the center of that first wall stud with its top edge just below the line you made to show where the shelf goes. When you have it where it belongs, mark where each hole is by running the point of a pencil around in it. Then you won't have to fuss if the bracket gets bumped out of place as you work.

Once you have the bracket where you want it, your assistant can hold it in place while you screw in the first screw. This is when you'll become fast friends with the cordless screwdriver or the drill motor. There are three holes in each bracket for the screws that attach it to the wall. Use all three. Install all the brackets for the topmost shelf.

Now take the shelf itself and lay it on top of the brackets. Center it and push it tight against the wall. Then start driving the ½-inch screws through the remaining holes in the brackets vertically into the shelf itself. Your assistant should push down on the shelf from above so you can get each screw started into the shelf. If your assistant can't push down hard enough, try having him or her put a full gallon of paint or some other fairly heavy item on the shelf above the bracket and push down on that.

If you still can't get the screw started into the shelf, you may have to use a drill or center punch to start each screw hole. If you use a drill, choose a drill bit the same size as the solid core of the screw—that is,

extra
brackets

not as wide as the threads. The easiest way to predrill is first to do the hole for the front screw of the first bracket. Then drill a hole for the front screw of the bracket at the other end of the shelf and drive home those two screws. Now it's easier to make the holes for the rest of the screws without getting the shelf out of alignment or wearing out your partner. Follow the same sequence if you use a center punch instead of a drill. Just try not to drill or center-punch your partner. Okay?

If you're using more than one piece of pressed board per shelf, install a bracket into the last two studs nearest the end of each separate piece of pressed board. This provides the extra support needed: As a shelf, two pieces of pressed board are a bit weaker than one. (See the illustration on page 99.)

Once you've finished the top shelf, start on the next one down. By now, most of the problems that are going to arise have done so. You've developed a routine, and the rest of the shelves should go in quickly.

STORAGE FOR GARDEN TOOLS

Unless you have other storage areas for your garden tools, you can store them on a wall of your garage with a specialized hook for each tool. First mount a 1- by 4-inch piece of wood on the wall at the height you want the hooks (try 5 feet). Carpenters call the 1- by 4-inch board a "ledger." It protects the wall and simplifies installing the hooks that come next. The length of the 1- by 4-inch ledger is determined by how many tools, brooms, etc., you will store here. Allow about 1 foot for each tool (or as little as 6 inches, if that's all the space you have). Stagger the height of the tools if you hang them with a 6-inch spacing. Install the 1- by 4-inch ledger the same way you put up the brackets: Just drive a screw through it at each stud, but predrill the ledger so you don't split it. Now you can install the hooks for the garden tools directly into the ledger.

STORAGE FOR LONG ITEMS

If you have some very long items to store that the hooks won't handle (e.g., pieces of lumber or pipe), install three large shelf brackets (the same type you used for the shelves) about 7 feet off the ground—high enough to keep most of us from hitting our head on them. Above the ledger or above your highest shelf are good areas to install these brackets if you have room in either of these places. Be sure the items you want to store here will catch on at least two of these three brackets.

Now that you know how, you can use these same instructions and materials to install the utility-closet shelves you've longed for ever since you moved in—or anywhere else in the house that needs them, for that matter.

HOUSEHOLD CLEANING SUPPLIES

What do you really need?

If you've got household cleaners stuck under sinks, in the garage, and maybe in a storage closet or two, most of those cleaners are nothing but clutter—especially if you have cleaners you've never even tried or that haven't seen the light of day in years. We have some very definite ideas about cleaners as items of clutter. We ought to: We use them all day long to clean about fifteen thousand homes a year. And we wrote two books on the subject: *Speed Cleaning*, for weekly cleaning; and *Spring Cleaning*, for the big jobs.

First of all, it makes much more sense to have one cleaner that does ten different jobs than to have ten different cleaners to do ten different jobs. Besides cluttering up the house with all those specialized cleaners, it takes more time and more money to purchase them originally, it's more complicated to replace them as you use them up, and the cleaning job itself takes longer when you're using different kinds of cleaners. How much better, simpler, and more efficient to carry just a few very good ones. We carry just one heavy-duty cleaner and one light-duty cleaner with us as we clean. For example, our heavy-duty liquid cleaner (we call it "Red Juice") is the best cleaner we've ever come across. It's nontoxic, odorless, and biodegradable. It's so safe it's been approved by the USDA for use around food. The most important thing, though, is that it works miracles on dirt, grease, and grime in every imaginable combination. We test products continually, searching for high-quality tools and products that are safe both personally and to the environment. If you would like to know more about the cleaners and cleaning tools we use that can help you weed out specialized, unused "miracle cleaners" that are cluttering up your house, please write or call us. We have listed both our address and telephone number in Appendix B, "Resources," at the end of this book.

We believe that cleaning supplies should be stored in their own eye-level storage space whenever possible. It's so much simpler to retrieve cleaners and replace them after use from such a cabinet than from the dark and crowded dungeon under the kitchen sink. That's one reason some of us never get around to cleaning: It's too much trouble to get the cleaners out of their hiding places. Many of us don't even know what's under there. Move the cleaners to "hotter" storage space and use the area under the sink for items you don't often use, or dedicate it to the garbage and recycling bins only. As we're cleaning, we carry our cleaners around the house in a special cleaning apron so we don't make numerous trips back and forth to this storage area. For more information regarding our specialized we-couldn't-clean-without-it apron, write or call us. (Once again, see Appendix B, "Resources.")

KEYS

How to avoid searching for the keys every time you want to leave the house.

This plan solves the problem of an absolutely needless and particularly exasperating waste of time. And it solves it so effortlessly that it may give you a bit of encouragement to tackle some of the more difficult clutter or organizational problems you're faced with.

All you have to do is mount a screw-in hook (or hooks, if others in the family need help also) close to where you normally end up when you're coming into the house. For many people, that's the kitchen. Or just inside the garage door into the house, or next to the burglar alarm. Usually the second choice of where to mount it is near where you exit— that is, just inside the door rather than where you usually head to in the house after entering. The drawback to leaving the key here is that often you have your arms full of groceries or something else as you enter the house so you can't put your key on its hook until after you set down your load. Now you have to walk back to your entrance point to deposit the key. Ultimately, where you install it is secondary. That it's convenient and actually used is what's important.

If the hook is going to withstand daily assaults, it's got to be mounted into something solid. Were it to come loose in a few days, with the track record some of us have, it may be a year before it's reinstalled. Try putting it directly into the molding around the door to the kitchen, for example. To avoid splitting the wood and to make it easier to install, predrill a hole slightly smaller than the hook. Don't put the hook directly into a door, even if the door is solid wood, because the keys will go flying when the door is opened or closed.

If you're installing a hook into gypsum board, install one that's long enough to sink into the stud at least ½ inch. (See "Garage Shelves," page 95, for how to find a wall stud.) The hook won't be secure enough if you screw it into just the gypsum board. If you have no other choice, first mount a piece of wood about 4 by 6 inches with toggle bolts or hollow wall fasteners (available at any hardware store). Then screw the hook into the wood. The wood will also prevent the paint on the wall from being scraped by the keys.

Some gift shops carry a wooden plaque with hooks for hanging keys. It may not be something that your decorator would choose, but that's an even easier option for key management if you do find one you like.

If you have problems finding your keys even after you've put up a key hook, you've probably installed the hook in the wrong place. Move it to a place you can't avoid when entering the house with the keys still in your hand. Consciously develop the habit of using the hook and it will become second nature.

LETTERS

Catching up on correspondence.

Household correspondence is best kept in its own file, of course, in chronological order or whatever other order makes sense for your needs (see "File Cabinets," page 84). But are you postponing writing letters to track down that magazine subscription that never came in the mail, or to complain about a defective product, or to commend that bus driver who was especially nice the other day? If so, and if you feel you don't have the time to deal with your correspondence adequately, then you might consider "boilerplate" letters.

By "boilerplate" we mean letters that are already substantially pre-written so that sentences or paragraphs can be incorporated in chunks from one letter to another. For example, if you often find yourself writing to order an item in the mail, you can set up a standardized boilerplate letter and use it over and over again for different correspondents. Just change the date, salutation, address, etc. They're especially useful for writing to your senator and congressperson: You don't have to scrounge around for their address every time you write, so you can pop off a letter of furious indignation with an ease that will startle your representatives.

If you have a home computer with a word-processing program, writing your own boilerplate letters is a project you might want to tackle on your own. If you don't want to take the time, or if you want help composing your correspondence, consider investing in one of the several in-print collections of standardized letters. One of these collections[1] has over eight hundred business and personal letters for almost every imaginable occasion: thank-you letters, apologies, complaints, congratulations, letters requesting favors, letters requesting information, fund-raising letters, invitations, etc. Use the letters as is, or modify them for your own application. We won't tell a soul where you acquired your newfound literary skills.

1. Harold E. Meyer, *Lifetime Encyclopedia of Letters* (Englewood Cliffs, N.J.: Prentice Hall, 1991).

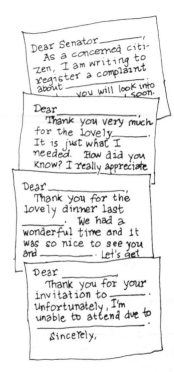

MAILING LISTS

Dealing with unwanted mail.

Mention unsolicited (mistargeted or "junk") mail and you'll almost invariably hear a chorus of complaints. I maintain that it's not all that much of a bother. Personally, I enjoy getting all sorts of mail—even mail I didn't request or expect. And the number of direct-mail pieces we receive each day is far outweighed by the number of TV, radio, magazine, and billboard ads we see and/or hear in the same period. Most of us have ordered something via the mail at least once: In 1990 almost 100 million people in the United States made a home purchase. And mail-order purchases have become more and more of a preferred option for those who want to minimize the environmental impact of making purchases: Better to have one delivery truck stopping at thirty houses than thirty cars fuming their way downtown so their owners can shop.

Consumers do have a say, however, in how their names and addresses are used in the marketplace. Senders of unsolicited mail are all too happy to cooperate with you if you don't want their mail: Mass mailings are quite expensive, and the sender is no more interested in mailing mistargeted mail than you are in receiving it.

There are two main strategies for reducing incoming mail at the source. The first is tell one or more specific companies directly that you don't want your name and address added to a list. Simply add a handwritten message to the bottom of business correspondence in which you give your name and address, such as when ordering merchandise, subscribing to a publication, making a donation to a charity, or entering a sweepstakes. Write something such as, "Please do not add my name or address to your mailing list." (Red ink couldn't hurt.) Initial and date it.

If you correspond with businesses that you *do* want to hear from again, but you don't want them to release your name to anyone else, alter your message a bit. Write something such as, "Please do not release my name and address to any *other* mailing list," or ". . . to anyone else," or ". . . to anyone's mailing list other than your own." That should do the trick. If you are speaking to someone rather than corresponding by mail, just ask the person if your name will be released to any list. If so, decide if you want to be excluded.

The second strategy for reducing national advertising mail at the source is to write to the Direct Marketing Association (DMA). They don't do mass-mailings themselves, but they do offer a free service, the Mail Preference Service (MPS), for those who want to eliminate their name from national advertising lists. Send them your full name and address—including the Zip code and any misspellings and commonly used variations in your name (e.g., R. Roger Clark, R. R. Clark, R. R. Clarke) or the format of your address (e.g., "71 Andover St., Apt. A" vs. "71A Andover St."). Make sure you give the name of the recipient of the unwanted mail (i.e., if the mail is coming to your husband, send them his name, not yours). Don't telephone: The DMA must receive this information in writing. The address is listed in Appendix B, "Resources," at the end of this book.

On a quarterly basis, the DMA sends out a list of people who have requested to be deleted from national advertising lists for many credit-card offers, free catalogs, sweepstakes offers, etc. Many national consumer direct-mail companies receive the DMA's deletions list and will remove your name. But don't expect a complete disappearance of unsolicited mail from your mailbox: Almost no *local* advertising firms receive the DMA's deletions list; it is for national lists only. And it will be a few months before it takes effect.

The DMA also has a service for those who wish to receive fewer telephone sales calls. Their Telephone Preference Service (TPS) removes your name from many national telephone sales lists at no charge. When you register with the TPS, your name and phone number are placed in a deletions file that is made available on a quarterly basis to participating national marketing companies. As with the Mail Preference Service, the TPS takes a few months to take effect and will not have an impact on local sales calls—just national. If you wish to register, write to the Telephone Preference Service at the Direct Marketing Association (the same address as for the Mail Preference Service), but state your full phone number, including the area code.

If you receive a one-time advertisement from a firm, it probably will do little good to write to them directly. Chances are that they bought the use of your name for a single time from a company specializing in mailing lists. When a firm buys a mailing list, it is entitled to use each name only once. So you would have to track down their original source, which is more difficult. But let's say you start being besieged with solicitations for a type of charity shortly after making a donation to a specific one. If you write directly to that charity and ask them to delete your name from any mass-mailing lists they had released, you might have greater success. The same applies to companies you regularly do business with, if you have reason to believe they are releasing your name.

If you are getting multiple copies of the same catalog, write to the catalog publisher directly. If the catalogs are addressed to a differently spelled name (e.g., one to "Jeff," another to "Jeffrey," and a third to "Jeffrey M."), be sure to tell them. Their computer thinks that three differently spelled names refer to three different people. Ditto if the address is spelled differently on the address labels. It's a good idea to mail them the actual address labels from the catalogs, because any coded information on them can help the company track down your name.

And then there are the hard-core tactics. For example, I heard of one fellow who used a different middle initial every time he subscribed, donated, or purchased anything in the mail. He kept a log of who got what initial. When he started getting unsolicited mail, he knew exactly where it was coming from by the initial. To us, that sounds like a lot more work than tossing the mail in the recycling bin.

MEDICINE CABINETS

What's lurking behind the mirror?

For some reason, medicine cabinets often function as a "Hotel California" for objects: They check in, but they don't check out. This is perfectly understandable, because all sorts of musty things can be hidden behind the mirror. But when the time comes for organizing it, here are a few ideas.

PRESCRIPTIONS

Fearlessly grab hold of every prescription bottle with an expiration date that has passed. Don't throw them away just yet—there are valid reasons for keeping a medical history. With it, for example, you can tell a physician which medicines have and have not worked for you in the past. Or it may be necessary to renew a prescription at some point in the future. So keep a record of the names and dates of the prescription medicines in the cabinet, but not the expired medications themselves or the hoard of cute but empty little bottles.

Transfer the pertinent information from expired prescription bottles to a summary file record. Keep this file in your household file cabinet. And record information in a table that looks something like this:

Patient	Date of ℞	Name & Dose	For	Doctor	Pharmacy & ℞ No.
Dad	12/1/91	Voltaren 75 mg. 2×/day	Muscle pain	H. Friedman	Cortese #282317

If appropriate, write a note next to the medicines indicating such things as effectiveness, side effects, or cost.

Once you've transferred this information to the table, throw the prescription bottles away. You're never going to find something to put in them, and if you throw them out you won't be tempted to store aspirin in a bottle labeled "Decongestant."

FRAGRANCES

Apart from the clutch of prescription bottles, the next most populous items in the medicine cabinet are likely to be all those half-empty bottles of cologne, perfume, and after-shave you cannot bear to part with. Trouble is—in addition to the lack of shelf space—if you keep them longer than their shelf life, you'll be flouncing about in public with rancid odors wafting from your otherwise delightful self. According to Steve Coffey, of the Fine Fragrance Group at Givaudan (a fragrance supply house in Clifton, N.J.), fragrances have a shelf life of about one year after being opened.[1] After a year, they begin to sour as the formula oxidizes in the bottle. Unopened, they may last two years. Lower temperatures slow down the rate of chemical breakdown of the fragrance, so refrigerated fragrances can last up to three years. It's also best to keep fragrances out of direct or indirect sunlight. So fragrances left out on a bureau or counter—especially near a window—are prime candidates for early souring.

Throw away bottles of fragrance you know you've had beyond their shelf life. And don't keep any more than you'll be able to use by the time they're due to sour.

If you get a bottle of fragrance as a gift and already have one or more opened bottles in use, store it in the refrigerator, where it is both cool and dark. (Keep the bottle wrapped in its original box, and store it out of the reach of children.) Avoid the freezer, however, because freezing may alter the chemical composition of the formula.

1. Deborah Bloomenthal, "Spring Cleaning: Medicine Cabinets," *The New York Times* (April 20, 1991), p. 16.

TOILETRIES

The shelf life of toiletries ranges from six months to several years. According to Dr. Gerald N. McEwen of the Cosmetic, Toiletry, and Fragrance Association in Washington, D.C., eye cosmetics (e.g., mascara) have the shortest life span.[2] Cosmetics with less water (e.g., lipstick) can last much longer. A shelf life of several years can be expected for toiletries such as mouthwash, toothpaste, Vaseline, shampoo, hair spray, suntan lotion, and rubbing alcohol. Newer lines of products (e.g., Coppertone sunscreens) stamp the shelf life on the product container itself.

No matter what the product, certain precautions will ensure the maximum storage life for the product. As discussed above for fragrances, store the toiletry item, wherever practical, in a dark and cool place. Wash your hands before dipping into an ointment, for example, that's going to be around awhile. Items mixed with saliva (e.g., mouthwashes drunk from the bottle, or eye cosmetics moistened with saliva) are naturally going to go bad a bit sooner. Items whose containers are left open and exposed to the air are also going to go around the bend that much quicker. Signs of decay include rancid odor, oil separation, flaking, and discoloration—although discoloration by itself doesn't mean the product has expired (especially for sunscreens).

Once you've removed out-of-date items from the medicine cabinet,

2. Ibid.

take aim at the newer but still unused ones, such as the greasy hair treatment that nobody in the household uses anymore, or the makeup that turned out to be a macabre color. Items in the medicine cabinet are probably more expensive per square inch than anywhere else in the house, but apply the same uncluttering rules here so you'll end up with things you actually use and enjoy.

Store related items on the same side of the medicine cabinet—especially if it has more than one door. This means that the hairbrush, hair comb, hair spray, hair spritz, mousse, hair color, and hair restorer all go on the same side. Likewise, keep together the contact-lens cleaner, the saline solution, and the lenses' storage case.

Also arrange the two sides with an eye toward the sequence in which you use the cabinet—especially if there are two or more doors on the cabinet. For example, if you take care of your hair first, then put on deodorant, and then apply a fragrance, store them in a logical sequence in the cabinet so you don't have to switch between sides. Organize what's left according to the guidelines in the section "Cupboards and Drawers," page 75.

NATIONAL GEOGRAPHICS

They seem to be everywhere.

Somebody should declare *National Geographic* the nation's official magazine. As of September 1991 there were approximately 3.784 *billion* copies of *National Geographic* in print, and just about every one of them is still in somebody's garage. It is such a splendidly photographed thing of beauty that we feel like criminals when we try to throw one away.

But as beloved as they are, the time comes when *National Geographics* need another home. Be generous. Be wily. Take the plunge. And be comforted by the fact that every issue you have is likely to be in the local library.

Not long ago, a reader wrote to the columnist who writes the consumer column in one of our local papers (Chris Bjorklund, "Consumer File," *The San Francisco Examiner*). She asked where she could take her old *National Geographic* magazines as well as their glorious maps. The columnist printed her request in the paper.

An avalanche of responses poured in, among which were the following:[1]

1. Chris Bjorklund, "Consumer File," *The San Francisco Examiner* (April 21, 1991), p. E-6, (April 28, 1991), p. E-6.

• Donate the magazines or maps to special education and English-as-a-second-language classes. Donations to public schools are tax-deductible if a receipt is requested from the school's administration—just as one would request a receipt for goods donated to a charity.

• Use the magazines or maps as wallpaper for a den, child's room, etc.

• Donate the magazines and/or maps to thrift shops.

• Donate the maps to the local friends-of-the-public-library group for their annual book sale to raise funds for the library. People love to buy the maps at book sales.

• Donate the maps to middle-school geography and history teachers, who love to get their hands on them for use as visual aids in the classroom. Some teachers have to buy their own teaching aids, and are quite grateful. Some schools may express an interest in the magazines as well.

So it sounds like your local school district is the first place to call to find a new home for your *National Geographics*—especially the maps. If you have trouble placing them, maybe you should write to the consumer column in your own local paper and broadcast their availability. You'll probably be inundated with responses. (The same applies to other things as well: Someone just wrote in and asked if anyone could use hundreds of five-gallon plastic drums. He'll probably hear from half the painting companies in town.)

We called the nice people at *National Geographic* to see if they had any other suggestions about what to do with a surplus of the magazine. They suggested that you contact local schools, libraries, jails, hospitals, nursing homes, and charitable foundations.

Lastly, a friend of mine donated a sizable book collection to a library in his overseas homeland via the local consulate. If you have a large collection of magazines, consider calling one or more of the consulates to see if they are interested in a donation of your *National Geographic*s. If you live too far away to deliver them in person, anticipate some expenses for packing and shipping.

PAPER

What to do with all the paper that slithers into the house.

You'd think that paper clutter would be easy to deal with. After all, paper comes boldly through the front door in broad daylight. It's not surreptitious, like a mouse. Actually, it's probably easier to get rid of the mouse—at least you can set a trap for it.

There's something about the importance of the printed word on paper that causes even the most conscientious among us to put off making a decision. When the mail arrives, we sort through it and then put it in a growing pile, even though we could have disposed of it just about as quickly by deciding appropriately right then and there. Make the first dent in the incoming flow of paper by reducing it at its source (see "Mailing Lists," page 108). The next step is to make the first sorting of incoming mail more useful: As soon as you pick it up, toss what you don't want or aren't interested in into the recycling or trash bin—not into a separate stack on the counter "for now." You're not going to experience an unexpected burst of interest in it later.

If you're any kind of American at all, there are undoubtedly several bills in your mail most days. Put those in your file cabinet in the "Bills" file as you come to them. If a piece of mail was an invitation addressed to you alone, decide then and there if you are going to attend, mark it on your calendar, and file the invitation in your monthly "Tickler" file. If the invitation is for you and your spouse, or if it includes the kids, put it on the dining room table and get an answer tonight at dinner. Then file it appropriately.

If you're lucky enough to get a real letter from a real person, read that correspondence and file it in your correspondence file. Put the interesting ads or magazines next to your chair in the living room and sit down to read them when you can.

If you don't even glance at some of the magazines you subscribe to, save yourself the guilt and the expense and cancel those subscriptions. The magazines coming in the house are chock full of articles that either look interesting to you or that you know you "should" read. They may make you feel like a failure because you almost never get around to them. Why put yourself through all that? If you cancel them, you'll shed the guilt and save a few bucks a year.

For the magazines you do look at, at least cursorily, tear or cut out interesting articles and recycle the rest of the magazine so you don't have growing piles of them all over the house. Put these saved but unread articles in your file cabinet in their own file and read them at your leisure—without the clutter of the rest of the magazine. The article file is fun to look through when you have time and are in the mood. You'll find some wonderful articles. But you'll also discover that many of them have since lost their appeal, and those you can toss more easily. Once you've read an article, toss it, give it to a friend, or file it in one of the permanent files you allow yourself for articles (e.g., "Cats," "Diet," "Garden," etc.).

None of us will ever discard all of our correspondence, but when you've answered a card or a letter, generally toss it. The same goes for Christmas cards. (They seem to be as difficult as *National Geographic*s to toss.) Update your own address book as necessary, and recycle the cards. Save those special letters from special people at special times in your life in a separate "Correspondence" file.

PHOTOGRAPHS

Organizing memories.

Here's an effective guide to reducing drawers full of photos. It will reduce those volumes of photos to a number and format that people may actually look at and enjoy. That was the whole idea in the first place, right? You'll not only be able to enjoy the photos again, you'll also be reclaiming all the drawer space they were taking up.

SUPPLIES

1. A tabletop or other large working surface.
2. A Rolodex-type photo storage unit, or several photo albums of your choice.
3. A video transfer system or service (optional).

The first step is to round up all your photos. As one storage place fills up, people start storing them in a new place, so investigate the house thoroughly. You'll need every last picture at hand to do this properly.

The idea is to edit your photo collection. Think of your photos as raw footage of a movie. If all the footage shot to make the movie *Cleopatra* were shown, the audience would expire from boredom. Likewise, your home photo collection is unedited, and the show is far too long and boring. People just won't look at them if there are too many photos per event. In the first packet of pictures, you may notice that of the thirty-four prints, twenty-seven of them are of your grandchild's second birthday party. Like most people, you have occasional gems interspersed in a much larger collection of more ordinary photos, plus repeats. Let's fix that. While we're fixing it, don't cause any damage to your photos unnecessarily. Keep your hands clean, don't handle the photos more than necessary, and there's no reason even to touch the negatives during this process.

If your collection consists of slides, use a light box that will allow you to view a number of slides at once. You don't need a fancy one: A cheap plastic fold-up model will do. Or you may be able to rent one. Except for how you view them, you'll edit them exactly the same as prints. With slides and home movies, pay particular attention to the video transfer option at the end of this section.

ORGANIZE

Once you've gathered together all the packets of photos, start by sorting them into chronological order. If you're lucky, the processing date is on the packets or on the back of the prints. The packets themselves may already be somewhat sorted chronologically by the way they were put in the drawers (i.e., the oldest ones are on the bottom). If this is true in your case, keep them in that same order. If you have absolutely no idea about the year of certain groups of photos, set them aside for now. Start a new pile whenever the one you've been working on gets too tall and unwieldy. Each pile should be arranged so the oldest photos are on top.

Once you've gone through them all, you'll have the photos, some still in their packets, arranged roughly by year. Now it's time to decide where to insert the photos you set aside earlier. After you've seen all the photos, sometimes your memory will be jogged and you'll now know where a stray group belongs. If you still don't know where some photos belong, consult other family members or friends. As a last resort, guess.

EDIT

Start with the oldest photos. Go through this first pile, one photo at a time. As you look at each photo, you're going to make an increasingly rapid editorial decision. Do you want to see this again? Do others? If yes, put it in the "keep" pile. If no, put it on the floor or in a trash can, but not back in the packet. You might as well place an empty trash can right next to you, because you're going to need it. Save the packets, with negatives enclosed, in chronological order for the time being.

When you come to several photos of one event, you not only have to decide which photos are keeps and which are discards, you also have to pick the best of the keeps. For example, you may have an entire packet of photos of Christmas 1972. Spread them all out on the table. Discard the obvious misses. Now pick the very best photo from those not discarded and put it in the keep pile. Then find the second-best picture on that same subject and put it in a separate "seconds" pile. Pick a third-best photo on the subject and put it in a separate "thirds" pile. *Throw away* any additional pictures of that same subject.

SHARE

Ultimately you'll keep the best photos for yourself and give the seconds and thirds photos to other family members or friends. If there are more than two such people living away from home, make a stack for each of them. If your kids are still at home, make collections of the seconds and thirds and save them for when they're older. Just never tell anyone which ones are seconds and thirds, so siblings never have an inkling that someone is getting preferential treatment. Set all the negatives aside for now, leaving them in their original packet and in chronological order.

By giving photos to people who don't live in your home, you will realize one very important benefit: In case of a disaster such as a fire or a flood, these second and third copies of your precious photos will survive because they've been sent elsewhere.

Let's be very clear by what we mean by saving just the *one* best photo of each subject for yourself. Let's say you have over two dozen perfectly good pictures of the aforementioned grandchild's birthday party, but you're going to save only the best one. Please don't start making smaller subjects so you can try to get away with saving more photos—pictures with others in them, pictures of the grandchild alone, pictures of eating, pictures of the games played, pictures opening gifts, etc. Just the best *one*. This child has his or her picture taken by you every year, and you take pictures at Christmas, Thanksgiving, the Fourth of July, Memorial Day, Labor Day, and one or two other occasions thrown in for good measure. If you keep just one from each of these occasions from birth until college age, you'll have approximately 150 pictures of this one child. That would fill several albums. You'll be satisfied.

If you have just one photo of a particular subject, it doesn't mean you can't toss it. For photos that are not repeats, ask yourself these questions: Do I know why the picture was taken? (A magnificent sunset, perhaps, but now that you've captured it on film, you realize you had to be there to enjoy it properly.) Do I even know what it is? (It's surprising how many photos are so obscure they're unidentifiable. Perhaps you were going through an artsy period with your camera.) Do I know who is in it? (If neither you nor anyone else in the household does, why memorialize them forever by including their photo in your collection?) As you've probably already guessed, toss these photos.

The flip side is also true. If you took twenty-five photos of the aforementioned sunset and not one of them was any good, don't automatically save a first, second, and third and add them to their respective piles. Instead, throw the whole batch away.

Ultimately you'll have three or so piles left (depending on how many piles you've been making to give away). By far the largest pile should be the one in the trash. Remember *Cleopatra*. Editing reduced the *Cleopatra* footage from hundreds of hours down to two hundred forty-three minutes. Something similar should happen when you edit your home photos.

Now send the copies to whomever you decided on. The photos you have left are in chronological order, changing subjects as they occurred, and you're all set to put them in the albums. Do it quickly before someone knocks over the piles!

IDENTIFY AND DISPLAY

As long as you've gone to all this trouble to get the photos edited and filed, take one more important step: Write the names of the subjects, the location, and the approximate date on the back of each photo you've kept. Most of us have old family photos that no one in the family can identify with certainty. The next generation to enjoy this wonderful album you are making will bless you for taking the time now to add archival information to the back of the photos. If you have slides, movies, or videotapes, make these same annotations.

There's another way of displaying photos that's convenient and very informal. It's a Rolodex-type file with a plastic protector for each photo.

It can be set on a table or shelf and is less imposing than bulky photo albums.

A third method of displaying your photos is to transfer them to a video format. If you already have the video camera, you can purchase a video transfer system for about $100. Or call a video duplication service and have them do it for you. This method is especially efficient if your collection is in slide form. It's so much simpler to view them via the VCR than with the slide projector and screen buried in the back of the closet somewhere. The same consideration should be given to home movies.

However, there are two disadvantages to transferring to videotape. The first is that you get a somewhat fuzzier image of your slides—not the crisp, sharp image you get from the slide itself. The second disadvantage is that the videotape can be damaged or broken more easily than the slides themselves. Videotape, even unbroken, doesn't last forever and may start to decay after a number of years.

THE NEGATIVES

Don't even try to edit the negatives. Just save them all as is. The simplest option is to leave them in their original packets, but number the packets sequentially (starting with 1 for the oldest) while you still have them in order. In the event you ever do duplicate them, you won't have to go through the chronological sorting again. Now put them all in a small box, mark the outside of the box, and put it away in the back of a drawer or closet. Better yet, put them in a home safe or a bank safe-deposit box. Alternatively, photo-supply stores sell translucent storage envelopes for negatives. They allow you to store them in a three-ring binder album or in your filing cabinet. You can identify negatives quickly, without handling them, by holding them up to the light. Remember to transfer any notes or identifying information from the packet to the sheet.

RECIPES

There's an easy way to manage them.

What about that mass of random clippings and notes that constitutes your collection of recipes (exclusive of cookbooks)? Driving you batty, eh? You're not alone. A friend of mine has recipes stuffed in cookbooks, half-sorted in envelopes, transferred onto 3- by 4-inch *and* 4- by 6-inch index cards (two different half-finished projects), and floating around on his bookshelves in a permanent holding pattern. (He rarely cooks, by the way.)

The alternative is refreshingly simple and can be used fast enough to lure even the most inveterate of clutterers into becoming more organized with their recipes. Set up fat three-ring binders loaded with plastic sheet protectors. A blank sheet of paper in each protector is a helpful background for the clippings you're about to add. Install divider sheets with tabs on which you have written sage words such as "Soups," "Chicken," "Desserts," and the like. When a new recipe leaps out at you from Wednesday's newspaper, just zap it into one of the sheet protectors. No tape, no staples, no retyping. Just pop it in.

One of the side benefits to this system is that when you turn to the appropriate section, you will probably discover you already had a recipe for Chicken Cacciatore. If the new recipe has an interesting twist, just annotate the existing recipe and toss the usurper. Or if the newer recipe is a low-fat variation, pop it in the sheet next to the traditional variation.

Another benefit of this system is that you can create some inventive categories for recipes, so you'll end up with your own customized cookbook. For example, you might have a category called "Romantic," or "Cheap," or "Dinner for Two," or "Fast," or "Tofu" (if you live in California).

Yet another benefit is that you can have a section called "Restaurants." At last! A place to keep all those stray restaurant reviews. (The alternative is to create a separate file for them in your file cabinet.)

Provided you don't get carried away, these binders can become Recipe Central for the kitchen—that is, you can refer yourself to cookbooks without rewriting the recipes for the binder. Just keep a handwritten list, in the front of each section, of favorite recipes in various cookbooks. For example, in the front of the "Desserts" section you might list "Meyer Lemon Mousse—*Greens Cookbook*, page 354" without copying out the recipe at all.

If the number of three-ring binders expands beyond one, make sure you label the spine so you can grab the right binder without the slightest hesitation. Anything that gets in your way might tip the balance in favor of stuffing the recipe in a more slothful place, so be alert.

RECORDKEEPING

Which records to save and how long to save them.

You may be storing decades of canceled checks, receipts, and assorted slips of paper only because of a morbid fear of the IRS. Like many of us, you're convinced you'll need all of those records in perpetuity to avoid problems in a tax audit.

TAX-RELATED RECORDS YOU SHOULD KEEP

No matter where you derive your income, keep the proofs of its sources. For most employees, it's a W-2 form and possibly the final paycheck stub. If your income is from retirement funds, investments, or other sources, the same holds true: Save the appropriate pieces of paper.

The flip side is deductions. We aren't going to delve too deeply into that subject. That's between you, the IRS, your accountant, and the Supreme Being of your choice. Whatever you deduct, however, keep a record of its origins. Standard categories of deductions include your home, dependents, contributions, medical and dental expenses, taxes, and interest. A canceled check may not be sufficient documentation (especially for charitable contributions). So keep the receipt, sales slip, or other documents. And get a signed and dated receipt for any cash payments claimed.

HOW TO ORGANIZE THE RECORDS

Establish a file for the current year. A suitable name for the tax file would be "Taxes 19——." In this file put all papers related to income and deductions for this year only. For example, this is the place to put your most recent pay stub or interest income statements, as well as any receipts or paid bills that may be deductible. Within this file, put a labeled manila folder or envelope for each type of income and deduction.

Keep a separate file ("Property") for the title and other documents pertaining to your home or other property. But use the "Taxes 19——" file for deductible interest on the mortgage loan. File papers in the "Property" file that contain basic information about your property or that will impact on taxes for more than one year. Use the "Taxes 19——" file for papers concerned with the current year only.

Besides the IRS, there's another good reason to organize these records into files. If you pass away and someone else must take care of your estate, you'll save yourself from being cursed in your grave by your survivor, executor, or the administrator of your estate.

CANCELED CHECKS

Your checkbook is a basic source for keeping a record of your deductions. But don't put the canceled checks themselves into the yearly tax file, even though you paid the receipts and bills in the file by check. Do, however, get into the habit of writing the check number on all receipts you put in the tax file. Current canceled checks themselves will be stored in your file labeled "Checking Account." Older canceled checks can be stored in a cardboard box in chronological order.

When your "Checking Account" file starts to bulge with many months of canceled checks, remove all but the last two months' worth to permanent storage in a cardboard box designed for canceled checks. Stationery and mailing stores sell dandy cardboard boxes that are made just for storing years of canceled checks. It's gratifying how much easier it is to store and retrieve checks when you use a box designed for them rather than using a cardboard box of whatever size you happened to have on hand. Stationery and mailing stores also have cardboard boxes that hold hanging files upright, like your file cabinet does. You could use one of those boxes for all previous years' tax files if your file cabinet is full. Look in the yellow pages under "Packaging Materials." These boxes are also surprisingly inexpensive. While you're at one of these stores, look for other boxes that can be helpful for your particular storage needs. There are specialized boxes for blankets, dishes, paper records of differing sizes, and many others. It takes up much less storage space when the box you're using is just the right size.

SUMMARIZING YOUR TAX RECEIPTS

Since clutterers have an innate horror of keeping track of receipts, go easy on yourself. Just pop them into the front of the "Taxes 19——" file or into a manila folder kept there marked "Receipts." Make sure this file is easy to reach: If you have to search for it, your resolve may fail and the receipt will end up in your checkbook, as a bookmark, or in little piles everywhere.

Every so often, sift through these loose receipts in the "Taxes 19——" file (preferably annotated with the check number) and sort them into their respective manila folders or envelopes. How often you do so depends in part on the amount of paperwork your financial affairs generate. Try to sort them monthly (when you pay your bills, perhaps) or at least several times a year.

As long as you're sifting through this fine collection of receipts, it will greatly simplify your life at tax time if you summarize them from time

EXPENSE SUMMARY: TAXABLE YEAR 19——

Date	To Whom	Enter Amount in Appropriate Category							
		Medical and Dental	Taxes[1] Paid	Interest Paid		Contributions		Miscellany[4]	
				H/P/I[2]	Amount	C/NC/V[3]	Amount	Explanation	Amount
/		$	$		$		$		$
/		$	$		$		$		$
/		$	$		$		$		$
/		$	$		$		$		$
/		$	$		$		$		$
/		$	$		$		$		$
/		$	$		$		$		$
/		$	$		$		$		$
/		$	$		$		$		$
/		$	$		$		$		$

1. Real-estate taxes, personal property taxes, etc.
2. Enter "H" for home mortgage interest, "P" for personal interest, and "I" for investment interest. These are reported on separate lines of IRS Form 1040, Schedule A.
3. Enter "C" for cash contribution, "NC" for noncash contribution, and "V" for volunteer expenses or travel (@ 12 cents per mile). These are reported on separate lines of IRS Form 1040, Schedule A.
4. Record expenses such as child and dependent care, child-support and alimony payments, union dues, subscriptions to professional journals, uniforms, tax preparation fees, etc.

to time on a form like the one shown on page 135—which you are free to photocopy for your own use.

For those with unusual returns, scrutinize your return from last year to determine what categories to use for your own unique summary. When tax time comes, you'll be able to tally up each column in a flash, making the task of calculating your taxes incomparably more pleasant. If you hire an accountant to prepare your return, you can present these summaries with a flourish and watch him or her burst into tears. One reason for the tears is gratitude; the other is that he or she won't be able to bill as many hours for the preparation of your return.

HOW LONG SHOULD YOU KEEP YOUR RECORDS?

Professionals know reasons for storing documents that mere mortals can barely imagine. They've experienced firsthand the trench warfare of audits, and they've held the hands of those who've lost money because they were unable to document certain expenses. So we've prepared the following cheery little summary based on the recommendations of accountants and auditors.[1]

The IRS's position, by the way, is that "Generally, your records must

---

1. Chet Currier, "What Not to Toss Out," *The San Francisco Examiner* (April 20, 1991), p. A-12.

be kept as long as they're important for any federal tax law" (IRS Publication No. 552, *Recordkeeping for Individuals*). There. Guess that's cleared up a lot, eh?

Document	Keep
Adoption papers	Forever
Bank records	Six years
Birth certificates	Forever
Canceled checks	Six years
Contracts	Seven years past expiration
Credit-card records	Six years
Custody agreements	Forever
Death certificates	Forever
Deeds	Forever
Divorce decrees	Forever
Health records	Forever
Home-improvement records	Until you sell the house
Income-tax returns	Forever
Insurance policies	Four years past expiration
Inventory of major personal property	Forever
Investment records	Four years after disposal
IRA records of contributions	Forever
Loan papers	Three years after final payment

Document	Keep
Marriage certificates	Forever
Mortgage papers	Three years after final payment
Owner's manuals	As long as you own the device or appliance
Passports	Forever (as a record of travel)
Tax records	Three years after due date
Tax records, if you did not report taxable income that was more than 25 percent of your total income	Six years after due date
Tax records, if fraudulent or false returns were filed, or if no return was filed (shudder) even though one was due	Eternity
Utility bills	Treat as tax records if making office-at-home deductions
Warranties	As long as you own the device or appliance
Wills	Forever

SHOPPING

Shopping made easy—well, easier.

The more efficiently you shop, the fewer trips you'll make to the store. Making unnecessary trips to the store is a form of disorganization in your life.

OFF-HOURS

Shop at off-hours. If you must shop on the weekend, be there when the store opens. It'll be just you and the sales clerks. Last year I went shopping on the Saturday before Christmas. I went to a shopping center with two of San Francisco's most popular stores and maybe a hundred others. The largest store was even having a sale. I arrived at the 9 A.M. opening time, and no other customer was in the store. It was a madhouse two hours later, but I was already finished. I also parked right smack in front of the store, which made carrying all that stuff back to the car more tolerable—especially since it was raining.

It's hard to buy groceries at off-hours when you have to go to the store after work to buy food for dinner that night—the same predicament many others are in. That's why the store is so busy during those hours, needless to say. Instead, try shopping after dinner the night before. The trip will take you half the time. And you'll buy less food on impulse, shopping on a full stomach!

Work toward a goal of shopping for food only once a week—every other week if you can. The secret is having a complete list when you shop so you don't miss an essential item or purchase unnecessary ones. Also buy in sufficient quantity. Let's talk about the list first.

LISTS

Before you go to the store, complete a list. We say "complete" because you should keep a note pad handy and add items as you become aware of them. Add items you use in quantity to your list when you open the next-to-last one from your supply of that item. Mayonnaise, ketchup, soap, and paper towels are common examples of what we mean. Don't wait until you open the last one or, needless to say, until you're out. That's the kind of mistake that'll force you to go to the store sooner than you planned.

Pads of paper are cheap. Thoughts are fleeting. So put pads of paper for lists (or ideas about other things you don't want to float away) in several places other than the kitchen. Put one in the bathroom, on the nightstand, in your car, or in your purse. If sensible, stop right in the middle of whatever you're doing to add an inspired addition to your list. Otherwise it's too easy to forget. Occasionally round up the lists from the other places and add those items to the master list in the kitchen.

It's much easier to complete your list if your cupboards are organized and you can see at a glance what's running low. If you need help organizing your cupboards and drawers, read the guide for organizing them on page 75.

Before you go to the store, arrange the list by group—so all the dairy items are together, for example—or by aisle (if you know your grocery store that well). It's too easy to miss items if you rely on the "cross off each item as you grab it" method.

Whenever you have to go to the store, be sure you also do anything else that needs attention while you're out and about. That's when those other lists will come in handy: the one in the bathroom about refilling the allergy prescription; the one in the bedroom to remind yourself to take the dress to the dry cleaner's for next week's dinner; and the list in the car, where you were when you remembered that the battery needs to be checked. Do all those things on this one trip even though it will take you twice as long. It will take four times as long if you make the trips separately.

QUANTITY

Buy in quantity. Don't do it to save money, do it so you don't have to run to the store, fight the traffic and crowds, and miss your favorite TV show. Don't limit buying in bulk to food items either. You'd be amazed at the number of people in line at the post office who have a stack of envelopes in hand and buy exactly the same number of stamps as envelopes. They mail them and leave the post office without a single stamp for a home inventory. I don't understand this behavior. I *hate* going to the post office. You can never tell when it'll be least crowded. Why would anyone put himself or herself through such time-wasting torture more often than necessary? Anytime you find yourself at the front of the line at the post office, buy several months' worth of stamps. Even a year's supply of stamps wouldn't be too much. One hundred stamps cost about the same as a bag of groceries. Stamps never expire, and you can store them safely in your file cabinet, where you can find them when you need one. Now you can even buy stamps by mail from the USPS. Ask them for an order blank.

The same goes for greeting cards. Keep an inventory the same way you would keep a supply of stationery for letters. Keep a supply of birthday cards, for example, and resist making innumerable shopping trips for each occasion as it occurs. Don't get carried away: Keep only reasonable amounts of extras. Storing three extra deodorants is more akin to the problem than the solution.

GRADUATE-SCHOOL SHOPPING

Those at the graduate-school level of shopping start their Christmas shopping in July, August, or anytime they happen upon a bargain or an item that would be just right for someone. The holiday season is entirely too busy a time of year as it is. You'll feel smugly organized if your shopping is at least partially finished by the time it arrives. And rightfully so.

When purchasing things for your home, try to imagine how they will look after being pawed by the kids or after sitting out for a few months. For example, consider the following:

- How will it look dusty, dirty, and fingerprinty? Some things look terrible (such as a glass table, or many small plastic items) unless they are sparkling clean.
- How will you clean it? Some things (baskets are an example) are difficult to dust.

If you ask yourself these questions, you will stop some clutter from ever making it through the front door.

TELEPHONE BOOKS

Customize them.

Be inventive with your telephone book. Don't just leave it the way it came from the phone company. Underline business numbers you use regularly. Circle personal numbers after you've looked them up. Annotate wherever you get the impulse (e.g., if the dry cleaner did a great job, scribble a note to yourself so you'll remember the next time).

Install tabs on the edges of important pages. For example, if you find yourself regularly scrounging for the page with the out-of-state area codes, attach a tab to that page. You don't need fancy ones: You can add a folded-upon-itself piece of transparent tape (a type that will accept ink):

Area Codes

Fairfax	415	La Mesa	619	— —
Fairfield	707	Lancaster	805	Area
Fallbrook	619	La Puente	818	Codes
Fillmore	805	La Verne	714	— —
Folsom	916	Lemon Grove	619	
Fontana	714	Livermore	510	
Fort Bragg	707	Lodi	209	
Frazier Park	805	Lomita	310	

Other tabs might go on the first-aid page, sections of the yellow pages you use often, the Zip code map, the yellow pages index, the city/state/federal section, etc.—in short, any page you can remember searching for in the past.

TELEPHONES

How to manage the telephone instead of the other way around.

You know how it goes: You think you've finally got a moment to yourself, and the phone rings. An hour later, when at last you've extricated yourself from the phone, it's too late to finish in the kitchen, start your correspondence, pay bills, or visit with the kids. So you go to bed, with the unsettling feeling that once again you didn't complete anything close to what you set out to do that day.

If your work requires you to use the phone, you've probably had some training in how to use it. It's only sensible to believe that some things you learned about telephone usage at the office would apply to the home. They do.

AVOIDING INTERRUPTIONS

Use your answering machine even when you're home, at least when you would just as soon not be interrupted or when you want to enjoy some precious peace and quiet. It seems as if the only time a phone isn't answered when people are actually at home is when they're in the middle of something behind closed bedroom doors, and even then they have to stop and think about it for a second. Only in dire emergencies does anyone have the right to demand your attention when you don't want to offer it. You're a busy person, and there is absolutely no need for you to drop everything you're doing every time the phone rings.

Managing your incoming calls doesn't mean you don't like the person calling, or that you don't think he or she is important. It's just that you have your own agenda, and you'll talk to the person when it's more convenient or when you have the time and enthusiasm to spare.

Some people are reluctant to use an answering machine because they're afraid they might miss an emergency or urgent call. But if you follow that line of reasoning very far, you'll be reluctant to go to the store or out to dinner for the same reason.

The same goes for important calls. The likelihood of getting such a call is outweighed by the certainty of the aggravation caused by slavishly answering every call. Besides, we're not saying that you won't return such calls promptly. All the messages are right there on your machine, and you can check them at will.

For the ultimate privacy, turn off the ringer (or unplug the phone if there's no switch) and turn down the volume of the answering machine. You can even put the answering machine on a pillow so you don't hear the "clunk" when it responds to a call. Obviously, an intermediate level of privacy is made possible by screening incoming calls. If someone calls whom you want to speak to, pick up the call and turn off the machine. Most people seem to be flattered if you do pick up. If you don't, they won't know if you're home anyway.

If the location of your answering machine is such that you have to go flying across the house to monitor it, consider having other phone jacks installed so you can move your answering machine to more convenient locations. For example, a jack near the door to the backyard can be very handy.

TERMINATING CALLS

When you do answer your calls, it's no crime whatsoever to tell whoever is calling that you're in the middle of something—or that you're just about to leave—and that you'll call him or her back. It's also nice to say when you'll call back. In fact, try to make all your calls at your convenience.

Naturally, you should vary these tactics to end a personal call if the caller keeps on gabbing. Traditionally, whoever calls is supposed to give the conversational signal that the call is coming to an end. But if that doesn't happen, speak your mind without feeling like it's a confrontation. Just say the truth: It's time for you to go. Even if a caller is particularly insecure, most can survive a gentle reminder of the realities (and the pressures) of time.

If you don't want to take calls but can't screen with the answering machine because of other household members, just ask them to take a message for you. There's no need to lie. But tell them exactly what to say: "Mom can't come to the phone right now. Can I take a message?" Or "Dad's in the middle of something. Can he call you back?"

If you don't want to listen to a sales call, don't feel bad about ending it. As soon as you know what type of call it is, interrupt, and in a calm voice say, "I'm sorry, but I'm not interested." Quietly hang up if the caller persists. Remain cool. But also note that you may have to interrupt the caller to get your message across. Take charge of the situation, end it quickly and with civility, and get back to whatever you were doing—unruffled. Since it seems impossible to stop these unsolicited interruptions, at least you've wasted the least amount of time because you don't have a long cool-down period before you can get back to what you were doing. (See "Mailing Lists," page 108, for information on how to remove your name from telephone sales lists.)

If, by chance, it's Mother Teresa herself calling for a contribution, ask her to mail the literature to you, give her your address (if she doesn't already have it), congratulate her on her fine work, then say good-bye and quietly hang up.

MOBILITY

Get a cordless telephone. It's a magnificent invention. You can stir the pot on the stove, move to a more comfortable spot, let the dog out, answer the front door, and relax on the deck all during the same phone conversation. This is what we all tried to accomplish with long cords, remember? Those were the cords that were so tangled they became functionally shorter than the regular ones. When they weren't tangled, they were stretched across the room so people were forever tripping over them and sending the phone flying. The cordless phone overcomes these drawbacks effortlessly.

As long as no one "improves" this phone by adding a picture so the other person can see what you're really up to, we think it's well worth the investment. And the latest models are substantially improved in performance from the earlier ones.

If your budget won't allow a cordless phone, at least move your phone or add an extension phone so it's conveniently located. If you have a phone at your desk, for example, you can often be doing other things while you're on interminable hold.

VIDEOTAPES

Reel storage solutions.

Videotapes can clutter a living room or entertainment area in no time—especially if you get behind in labeling them and if you're taping programs far beyond a human being's reasonable capacity to watch them. Here are few steps you can take to straighten out the cassette mess.

This anticlutter project involves a couple of technical considerations to be observed. First, videotapes (and audiotapes, for that matter) should not be shelved or stored flat for any length of time—the spool of tape should be positioned vertically. After a few days, tape stored flat

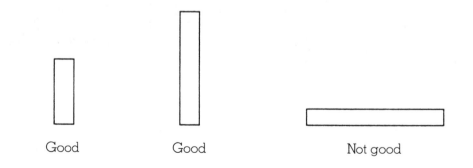

Good   Good   Not good

can settle on the spool unevenly—especially the outer edges—due to gravity. (But then, I'm settling unevenly around the outer edges, too. Life's like that.)

If the tape is loaded unevenly on the spool, it may be fed across the heads of the VCR unevenly as well. This can cause the playback picture to deteriorate in quality or to disappear altogether.

Luckily, if the tape has become uneven, there's a simple solution: "Repack" the tape by fast-forwarding it and rewinding it back to the beginning. This will respool the tape in an even manner. Repacking loads the tape to the exact tension at which your particular machine operates, so the quality of the recording will be at its optimum.

The second technical consideration is that tape in storage is vulnerable to all sorts of things: moisture, dust, sunlight, heat, etc. Moisture is especially nasty for tapes: When moist, the tape's surface emulsion softens and can be literally scraped off when the tape passes over the VCR heads. Not only are the heads clogged (they can be easily cleaned) but the tape can be permanently damaged as well.

The solution is to store videotapes, when not in use, in airtight cases.

The least expensive option is to be diligent about putting the tape back into the cardboard (or preferably plastic) sleeve that originally came with the tape. Such sleeves leave one side exposed to the elements, but unless you park them next to an open window or shower, you're probably not doing any significant damage to the tape. Video engineers are rather hard to pin down on this subject, however.

The preferred option—and the one elected by just about every video professional—is to store recorded tape in airtight plastic cases. These will protect tapes from deteriorating influences as well as anything short of storing them in a vacuum. In addition, they offer the advantage of making the tapes uniform in appearance on the shelf. Tapes tucked away in a drawer present no aesthetic dilemma, but they can look disorderly on an open exposed shelf unless stored in uniform cases. The one drawback of video storage cases (besides the slight added expense) is that they may be too wide to fit into a storage rack you may already have. But once in cases, tapes stand on their own more easily (like books), so a rack may not be needed.

The speed of deterioration of the tape also depends on the quality of the tape as well as the conditions of storage. Naturally, the cheaper the tape (in general) the faster the deterioration. Again, it's hard to be specific—but if your tape is over seven years or so old, it's in the danger zone. The "pro" lines of tape will usually last longer, but even they must eventually be transferred to fresh tape after several years. Unfortunately, the way to tell is almost after the fact: When you play a tape that's too old, you'll behold a virtually immediate, massive, and stomach-wrenching clogging of the heads as the old emulsion is scraped off by the heads.

The next task for decluttering your videotapes, now that you have them repacked and possibly ensconced in cases, is to label them. We all know how easy it is to amass a pile of tapes that have any number of movies or programs recorded on them, but we somehow didn't stop to label them and now nobody has the foggiest idea of what's on them. It's too much of an ordeal to review the tapes, so we set them aside and start in on new ones. Not only is this an expensive habit but also the shelves are bulging at the seams with unidentified tapes.

There are several steps you can take to make headway here. First, have a stack of Post-Its (or something similar) and a pencil right next to the VCR. When you start the recording, stick the Post-It on the VCR itself or the tape case to remind you of the program. Then just slap the Post-It on the tape as soon as you eject the tape from the VCR. If it's a keeper, transfer the information to the tape's own label.

If you record several programs or movies on one tape, be systematic about how you're going to find the beginning of each segment. We all know how annoying it is to scan through the tapes—not to mention the needless wear and tear that's being added to the machine. We suggest you write down, on the label, the start time of each segment (e.g., 20:32)—*not* the number on the four-digit counter (e.g., 1278). Different machines have different counter rates, so if you trade in your VCR for a new one or play it on someone else's machine, the counter numbers will be useless. On the other hand, most machines have compatible hour/minute/second recorders. If you didn't record the running times when you did the original recordings of movies, don't spend half your free time retiming everything. Rather, invest in one of the paperback movie guides that usually (check!) list total running times. Then just write down the total time next to each segment.

APPENDIX A: PRODUCTS LIST

The past few years have seen a proliferation of devices to help you combat clutter. Here's a quick list to help give you ideas for your own home. But we're a bit nervous about listing them. It's important to remember that these gadgets should be used for storing and organizing items that are left over *after* you've uncluttered your home. Don't use them to store stuff you shouldn't keep in the first place! Keep the Uncluttering Rules in mind at all times as you sally forth into this domain.

- Pot-lid racks
- Slide-out baskets
- Slide-out shelves
- Slide-out trash cans
- Under-shelf baskets
- Carry-all trays
- Recycling bins
- Spice racks
- Wall grid racks
- Cork memo strips
- Tie organizers
- Belt organizers
- Scarf organizers
- Coat/hat hooks
- Cedar closet organizers
- Cedar storage boxes
- Cedar sweater racks
- Under-bed storage chests
- Closet garment bags
- Hat boxes
- Silver storage bags
- Silver drawer-liners

- Closet accessory cases
- Shoe drawers
- Shoe racks
- Cosmetics organizers
- Jewelry cases
- Jewelry display cases
- Shower shelves/caddy
- Tub caddies
- Towel racks
- Corner shelves
- Laundry bins
- Garment racks
- Mesh laundry bags
- Over-the-door hooks
- Over-the-door ironing board
- Over-the-door pantry racks
- Document storage boxes
- Magazine racks
- Plastic-bag storage unit
- Vacuum accessory racks
- Stackable storage bins
- Newspaper racks
- China cases
- Multitier cabinet organizers
- Drawer organizers
- Key cabinets
- Compact-disc racks
- Videotape racks
- Audiotape racks
- TV remote-control caddy
- Photo albums
- Print/negative cases
- 35mm slide cases
- Magazine cases
- Firewood racks
- Bicycle racks
- Garment racks
- Multidrawer parts cabinet

APPENDIX B: RESOURCES

Cleaning supplies and techniques: Hopefully, decluttering will be the first step toward being able to keep your home not only organized but clean as well. Our company, The Clean Team, is San Francisco's busiest and most popular housecleaning service. Our first book, *Speed Cleaning* (New York: Dell, 2nd ed., 1991, 194 pages, $5.99) presented our own method for weekly household cleaning using economy-of-effort principles to cut your housecleaning time to a minimum—so you can move on to other things in your life. Our second book, *Spring Cleaning* (New York: Dell, 1989, 191 pages, $5.95), tackled the heavy-duty jobs that arise less often—such as stripping floors and washing windows—but that can't be ignored forever either. Both are available from your local bookstore or by mail at the address following. We'd also be pleased to send you a free catalog describing the time-saving cleaning supplies and equipment The Clean Team itself uses each and every day.

> The Clean Team
> 2264 Market Street
> San Francisco, CA 94114

If you're in a hurry, call us at 1-415-621-8444 and we'll mail you one the same day.

Mailing lists: To request that your name be removed from national advertising mailing lists, send the name, address, and Zip code—in writing—of the person receiving the mail to the address below. Make sure to include all variations in the spelling of the name and in the format of the address.

> Mail Preference Service
> Direct Marketing Association
> 11 West 42nd Street
> P.O. Box 3861
> New York, NY 10163-3861

Procrastinators: If you feel yourself deeply enmeshed in procrastination, fortunately there are at least two excellent books that can help you break the cycle of postponement, resolution, failure, and self-criticism in which you find yourself. If you don't alter the cycle, you're still in it. The following paperback books offer ways to step out of it.

Albert Ellis, Ph.D., and William J. Knaus, Ed.D., *Overcoming Procrastination: How to Think and Act Rationally in Spite of Life's Inevitable Hassles.* New York: Signet, 1977. 180 pages. $4.50.

Neil Fiore, Ph.D., *The NOW Habit: A Strategic Program for Overcoming Procrastination and Enjoying Guilt-Free Play.* Los Angeles: Jeremy P. Tarcher, 1989. 201 pages. $8.95.

Albert Ellis is one of the historic figures in the American school of psychology. The book by Ellis and Knaus presents specific, practical techniques developed by Ellis's school of rational-emotive therapy, which challenges the belief systems that maintain self-destructive and self-deceptive behavioral habits. They describe simple self-administered rewards and punishments to relearn patterns of behavior. Fiore is a licensed psychologist on the staff of the University of California, Berkeley. His book offers positive, practical techniques for breaking down one's identity as a procrastinator and reestablishing productive behavior.

Telephone sales calls: To request that your name be removed from national telephone sales lists, send the name, address, Zip code, and full phone number (with area code)—in writing—of the person receiving the phone calls to the address following. Make sure to include all variations in the spelling of the name and in the format of the address.

Telephone Preference Service
Direct Marketing Association
11 West 42nd Street
P.O. Box 3861
New York, NY 10163-3861